Men Are
Just Desserts

Men Are
Just Desserts

SONYA FRIEDMAN

WARNER BOOKS

A Warner Communications Company

Warner Books, Inc., 666 Fifth Avenue, New York, NY 10103
W A Warner Communications Company

Book Design: *Judy Allan*

Printed in the United States of America

First printing: May 1983
10 9 8 7 6 5 4 3 2 1

Library of Congress Cataloging in Publication Data

Friedman, Sonya.
    Men are just desserts.

    1. Women.   2. Men.   3. Autonomy (Psychology)
4. Intimacy (Psychology)   I. Title.
HQ1154.F75   1983   305.3'1   82-61881
ISBN 0-446-51255-9

To Uncle Jack, just because . . .

To Dr. Leah Hecht, whom I met at fourteen, long before she became my mother-in-law, and who said yes to success and education while so many others were saying no. To my husband, Dr. Stephen Friedman, who said, "I always knew you had potential," and who has supported my attempts to live up to it. To my now adult children, Sharon and Scott, who have always made me feel they were proud to have me as a mother. To Diane Braun, my right hand for the last seven years, who made me feel good on the most down days. To C. B. Abbott, who took my assorted ramblings and made them readable on paper. To Dr. Andy Yang, Dr. Bill Baker, Phil Bergman, Henry Baskin, and Alan Frank, who have generously and gracefully helped guide my career. And to the thousands of men and women who have shared their lives with me. I hope I have told your stories as you intended them to be told.

Table of Contents

*Men Are
Just Desserts*

Introduction

By the time I was twenty-one years old—a working mother supporting a family, married to a man going through medical school—I knew that growing up to get married wasn't the answer to all of life's problems. That revelation changed the course of my life, even though it took many years for me to act on it. Though I was still at the stage of searching for the course my life would follow, I was sure of one thing: The best a woman could ask of herself was to develop an ability to take care of herself.

The pleasures of marriage are often accompanied by resentments, by disappointments, by burst balloons—and by the end of the fantasy (which usually fades rapidly) that a man will transform one's life and give it shape, substance, and infinite security. Most of us can handle the news that our men, over a period of time, fall from grace and may have fits of bad temper, become ill when we need them, and shed many a tear for a dollar spent. Much more problematic to deal with is the truth that no man can give a woman her life or live it for her. Only she can do that for herself. To live our own lives with control and direction means an end to the fantasy of being cared for and the beginning of the reality of taking care of ourselves. A new reality, by the way, to rejoice in.

Many of us look to our pasts and hold up reasons why we have difficulty in being autonomous. The most common plaints are: "I am who I am and I can't change," and "I wasn't raised to do anything but care for others." Life is a matter of perceptions. When you're an autonomous adult, you can scrutinize the limitations and shortcomings of the past and come to different conclusions. Often, what we have considered as our early undoing can appear in another perspective as an asset. Let me give you an example.

My parents divorced when I was very young, and I really didn't know my father until I reached forty. I went to visit him with the intention of reconciling all the real and imagined hurts he'd inflicted on me. Our meeting yielded a fascinating tidbit: He told me that when I was three years old, he'd taken me out for the day. We were waiting for a bus on a Brooklyn corner and I was holding his hand. The bus stopped and I held on tighter to his hand to lift myself onto the first high step. My father told me he had let go of my hand and said, "If you want to get on this bus, do it yourself. Come on—you do it." I had looked shattered by this lack of support, he said, but I managed to clamber onto that bus. My first reaction to this story, as a forty-year-old professional woman, was unspeakable fury. How could he not help a three-year-old with such a simple task? Unconsciously, I'd probably held on to this early incident and carried it with me in anger for the following thirty-seven years.

When I left my father's house, the message of that anecdote hit me: Letting my hand go was probably the greatest gift he could have given me. At age three, I couldn't interpret it so generously, but its meaning obviously left an indelible impression on me. If you want something, my father was saying in his way, go after it yourself. Understand that you will always have one person upon whom you can depend—yourself.

The concept of *Men Are Just Desserts* springs from an attitude all women experience at one time or another: that of blaming men for what's wrong with their lives, and as a result, *not* doing for themselves. Once I was among these women. I blamed not only men but my home life, my mother, my friends, and—not least of all—fate, for not providing what I wanted. I was twenty-one when a light went on in my mind that illuminated a path for me toward autonomy. I asked myself questions: What was I going to contribute toward my life? What would I do to enrich my life and enhance the lives of those around me? Was I going to be stuck in the past and live according to someone else's plans, rules, and orders, or was I going to formulate a future that would work for me? How could I best do what I wanted and still have a solid marriage and healthy children? I was lucky. I found the way that was right for me.

The purpose of this book is to help you find the way that's right for you. By examining the messages that your parents delivered to you, by trying to comprehend the complexity of your relationships with parents, lovers, and husbands, you will, I hope, gain greater insight into who you are. You'll see how letting go of negative perceptions of yourself and replacing them with positive ones can create conditions where you *can* do for yourself.

Men have often been told, "Take a wife, but don't make her your life." When men are just desserts—that is, when a man is an enhancement to the already complete and satisfying life of a woman who makes choices and takes action—you will be able to choose a partner without surrendering who you are. Most of all, when men are just desserts, you may choose to be in the arms of a man, but need never fear falling into his hands.

Chapter One

Men Are Just Desserts

It seemed to me that there were two of me. One figure the sensible middle-aged woman with a family, with ties of the most ordinary and pleasurable kind, a family whom she loved, longed to make happy; a person well-dressed, normal, healthy. But someone else was in the background, a restless person, a lonely, selfish, weak person with violent desires and wild dreams of impossible things.
—Barbara Goldsmith, *quoting Gertrude Vanderbilt Whitney in* Little Gloria: Happy at Last

If I hadn't had to earn my own living, I would have been content not to amount to a row of pins.
—Helen Lawrenson, Stranger at the Party

Most of the novels I read ended in marriage and a blissfully happy state of which there was no more reason to write. . . . I was deeply impressed by the injustice [of marriage] for women, and putting it together with the story of my father and mother, I decided then and there that I would live to fight against marriage and for the emancipation of women and for the right for every woman to have a child or children as it pleased her, and to uphold her right and her virtue.
—Isadora Duncan, My Life

5

A few years ago I was sitting in a church, listening to a well-intentioned minister sermonizing to a young couple about to take their marital vows. Most of the sermon was addressed to the bride. She was told, in no uncertain terms, that she was to cease being Jane Roberts from that day on and become Jane Brooks. Everything that was associated with being Jane Roberts, the minister intoned, she must discard from that day forward so that she would thenceforth be recognized as Mrs. Richard Brooks. By assuming her husband's name, she would be subsumed into another identity. These two would share one name, one bedroom, one purpose in life, and cleave unto each other in this exalted "oneness." The word *individual* was to be unknown to her, especially if it referred to her.

I was getting restless. The message this particular minister was stressing made me angry. Why this belaboring of oneness—that loss of a woman's selfhood for a man's advantage? It is a message that can only overshadow the true one, which has to do with the importance of personal growth within a marriage by two people who, as separate individuals, reach for a common goal.

Every woman who agrees to this ideology of oneness will spend her life as someone else's person, not as her own. She will never quite know who she is. The trappings of oneness have built into them frustration, dependency, disappointment, and a ceaseless need for approval from the "one" a woman has become a part of. Oneness may sound romantic, but it is transformed into a grim reality after the magic of the ceremony has faded.

Give a man top priority in your life—make him the main course—and chances are you will lose not only your self but your self-esteem. Worship a man just because he *is* one, and you will subjugate yourself to him and wait, like a child, for his praise. Decide that you are nothing without a man, and this will become a self-fulfilling prophecy.

Consider a man just dessert—the reward for becoming an adult woman who is self-directed and emotionally grown up—and life will be all it can be for you.

Every woman has an obligation to make herself economically and emotionally independent before she chooses a mate. If a woman believes that a man will provide what she herself lacks—decisiveness, courage, economic security, access to achievement, personal gratification—she may well be disappointed. By establishing a man as the sole purpose in her life, she cheats herself of ever developing her own strengths and abilities. She becomes, then, not a sharing partner in a marriage but a dependent, a victim—and sometimes a victimizer.

The woman who has learned to care for herself may then seek out a man who will be the *reward* for the completion of her mission—that is, the dessert. Such a man will be an enrichment, an addition, and will provide a lovely place to lie at night, but he won't be the main course. No man is going to make you happy or give you a purpose in life—*you are.*

How do we give power over to men and make them the main course? We believe that this is appropriate behavior, what has always been done by women. And it's not only the traditionalists who are suffering from the "oneness backlash." Listen to the bind this woman is in. . . .

Linda is a strikingly attractive brunette who earns about $60,000 a year as a corporate executive. Divorced, with no children, Linda is involved in an affair with a man who pops into town once or twice a month. What started out as a friendship has deteriorated into an insulting, frenetic encounter.

"The last time we saw each other," she reported, "Jack was late getting out to catch his plane. I called the next day to see if he'd made the flight. He told me he had missed it and added, 'What a wasted evening.' There was no question in my mind that he was implying I'd intruded on his schedule and was also an inconvenience because he had to wait for the next flight. He regretted the hour and a half lost from his work, rather than regretting that we couldn't have spent that extra time together.

"I'm walking down the same old road," she continued glumly. "I thought I could be casual about sex, but I can't. Worse, I find that I'm still like a teen-ager, waiting for his phone calls, brooding that he's not around, feeling empty when he leaves. I'm settling for a lot less than what I should be getting."

Linda is one of the New Womanhood disciples who has looked at her sisters locked within the confines of their homes and vowed, "This won't happen to me." But the feeling of incompleteness without a man is just as strong in her as in the woman who admits to the feeling and *has* a man. Linda has changed her economic base—she has *achieved,* by anyone's standards—but emotionally she's bound to a destructive pattern by giving men responsibility for how she feels and making men the main course.

Consider Anna. Fifty-five years old now, Anna married

young—a beautiful, sweet-tempered girl from a working-class family who "blessed" her family by marrying a doctor. A year later she had a child. Four years later the marriage ended and she courageously got a divorce. She considered going back to school to learn accountancy, but her family objected—her clerical job was good enough. "Get married," they warned her, "and marry someone fast, before you're too old and your daughter's too grown up, or no man will want you."

Brainwashed by her parents' fears for her being alone, and displeased at not having the career she sought, Anna remarried. She convinced herself that she loved her husband and, for him, gave up her job. Within three years she had two more children. Her sweet temper, whatever remained of it, was never witnessed by her children or her second husband. She had a man, but again, the wrong one. And she didn't have herself. She didn't know what she wanted now, nothing made her content; she was an inept housewife and mother who felt unappreciated and unloved. She couldn't communicate with her family, except through rage. She belittled her children, scolded her husband, and bemoaned her fate: "Why me?"

Now in her middle fifties, she fears that her husband will leave her. She frets when he leaves the room she's in, panics when he goes to work. In her disheveled state she can no longer care for her house, her husband, or, least of all, herself. She believes that life dealt her a crippling blow.

Without the capacity and opportunity to learn how to care for yourself emotionally and financially, you are a prisoner of another's whims and fancies. If a woman, as in Anna's case, wants to toss away her options, she should realize that she does so at the risk of giving herself over to a man. Her parents told her she was nothing, a failure, invisible, without a man. Fulfillment, they said, was to come to her through marriage, not through her own strivings.

SITTING DOWN TO THE MAIN COURSE

Too often, women marry to escape their true selves, believing that marriage will make life work for them. Operating under the assumption that they are incomplete, unformed, lacking the capacity to take care of themselves financially or emotionally, they seek out a man who will be caretaker, benefactor, lover, and hero—"everything" to them. So, if a woman marries because she sees herself as incomplete—the lesser half seeking its greater half—a man will naturally seem to be instrumental in completing her.

Marriage is wonderful in its way, but this sanctified union should offer a woman freedom rather than enslavement to the destructive principle of "completion." We have been taught that we're not worth much—not a "real woman"—unless we prove our value by marrying. Frequently, our choice of a husband leaves us with little more than the feeling we started with: that we're not highly valued. What happened? Why didn't marriage make us happy? Where did all the frustration come from? What went wrong?

By developing only a small part of herself, a woman rushes toward marriage and surrenders to a man. By giving up her goals so she can provide support for his aspirations, she allows her life to revolve around his interests, needs, and purposes. In return for this tending to him, she expects devotion, respect, attention, and wedded bliss. Things don't work out quite so neatly. In many cases, her husband doesn't live up to her expectations of who he is and who she'll be in his life. She becomes angry, but even more fearful of abandonment. To reassure herself that she has, indeed, fulfilled her role as beneficent wife and loyal supporter and that he won't leave, she demands more acknowledgment from him, and perhaps doesn't get it.

Neediness produces vulnerability, and that vulnerability can create greater dependency. So if you feel you need a man to assure you that life is meaningful, stop now. It's time to reassess your skills, your personality, your self-esteem. The truth is, *the more you are, the less you need.* The more you are, the more you possess yourself without getting caught up with pleasing others and the more you can understand that no one's going to make you happy, or complete, but yourself. The more you *are,* the more you will realize that a man can detract from or enhance your happiness, but he can never be responsible for answering all your needs. The more you *are,* the more you see that he is not the main course—you are!

When I say, "men are just desserts," I am also using the word in another sense—"deserts," spelled with a single rather than a double *s:* You get the man you deserve. In my opinion, men don't select their life partners, women do. Oddly enough, women choose the wrong man over and over again because of what they are not, as opposed to what they are.

If you think you're only half a person, chances are you won't find a man who's a person-and-a-half—which will add up to the two of you. You'll select another half-person. If you estimate your worth at nothing, the man you choose, despite

11

his brilliant package, will, under all the natty dressing, smooth charm, and bravado, be nothing. Think of yourself as someone who will spend her life struggling, and the man you select will oblige you. Consider yourself someone who must suffer from emotional neglect, and no matter how you protest that it's intimacy you want, the man you marry will be delighted to stay as he is for you—distant. Think of yourself as a helpless creature who needs a strong shoulder to lean on, and you'll find yourself cuddling up to an overbearing tyrant who insists that all your decisions will be his—including the shade of your pantyhose and when you should wear them.

RULE FOR LIFE NUMBER ONE: *You marry at the level of your own psychological health.*

Strive though you will to find someone who possesses the strengths you lack, you will ultimately wind up with a man who's approximately your double. What are you missing? Most women bounce from crib to school to college (if they're lucky) to a quasi-career, then into a connubial bed, without first defining who they are. Their totality depends on their getting a husband.

Defining yourself means asking these urgent questions: Who am I? What are my pleasures? What are the things that give me pain? What do I have in life to work with? What are my abilities? What do I want as a goal, and what process should I use to reach it? Can I let go of old bitterness toward my parents and accept them for who they are? What characteristics of my own personality need work? How do I repeat self-destructive patterns? Can I learn to stop them?

Dr. Albert Ellis, in *Reason and Emotion in Psycho-*

therapy, lists twelve important self-defeating beliefs that prevent us from defining ourselves clearly and becoming adults. Among these, the following are critical:

- "It is terrible when things are different from what I would like them to be."
- "My suffering is caused by others and events beyond my control."
- "It is easier for me to avoid than to face up to difficulties and responsibilities in my life."
- "I can become happy without taking action on my own behalf."
- "I have little control over how I feel."

These five beliefs all share a common basis: "I have little or no command over my life and must or should adhere to others' notions of who I am and how I should live my life." But responsibilities and difficulties do not disappear through denial or evasion. Happiness is not dispensed to you. As Eleanor Roosevelt said, "No one can make me feel inferior without my consent."

The happily-ever-after of marriage doesn't work, does it? Happiness means nothing, because we haven't given anything to ourselves within the marriage other than expectations of the "someday" dream. Someday I'll have everything I want. Someday my husband will change. Someday I'll be really loved. Someday I'll be somebody, and everyone will notice.

The phrase "men are just desserts" does *not* reflect a disparaging view of men at all. It's not meant to diminish a man, nor to detract from his importance or good qualities. Rather, it is meant to give him credibility by encouraging you to learn to see him as he is, not as you wish he were. If he too is incomplete, then both of you can begin to grow to person-hood. "Men are just desserts" is a phrase meant to remind us that a man is not the main course, someone around whom a woman's life must revolve. If you make dessert the mainstay of your existence, you fill up on empty calories and become fat, lazy, careless, and addicted to self-destructive patterns. You're going to be psychologically and physically unhealthy. When a man takes an overly significant role in your life, you lose your true self in trying to please him. Make a man the focus of your attention, and you'll always be angry that he isn't doing the same for you!

The worst "words to live by" that a parent can present to a daughter are: "Love is the entirety of a woman's life, but just a small part for a man." Indicate to a daughter that she's to look forward, generally, to a master/slave relationship, and you're asking her to trade off her life for his and make him the main course.

The scenario for making men the main course takes many forms, but this one is typical. Many women select hus-bands when they're in their teens. A decision is made to get him through school, work for a while, establish him in his business, then stop working because "his wife doesn't have to work."

A man is out there, meeting people, starting to explore op-portunities, encountering situations he has to cope with on an adult level. His wife is still in the background, caring for him. If they've got a child and he's studying or involved with paperwork in the evenings, she must stay carefully out of his way. Unable to interact with him or discuss some of the events in her life, she must be content with the meager few hours of his attention he doles out—rarely undivided, since he's preoccupied with his tasks. She feels like an intruder in his scheme of things. The loneliness begins to wear on her. But what can she say? He's trying to make it for both of them.

A man may be propelled in a straight-line progression to a measure of success; meanwhile, his wife is still where she was when she met him at the age of fifteen or sixteen—a little girl, really, who hasn't honed the skills or developed the self-confidence that result from experience gained in the world. She hasn't the wherewithal to care for herself should something happen to her husband or their marriage.

As a man grows in his profession, he's home less and less, and delegates more chores to his wife. Because a wife in this situation has no life outside her home, she can't say, "Let's share this chore together, or you do it. I have important things to do, too." Rankled, he will answer, "And what's that? What do you have to do all day *but* chores?" Then it happens.

He may find his secretary or a woman associate ever more attractive, because she understands his life more fully. She becomes his daytime partner and more his wife; his wife becomes more like a stranger who gets a weekly household salary. So he leaves his wife for the other woman. The wife, stunned, angered, and hurt, is suddenly left on her own, with no saleable skills with which to provide for herself. They may have been married, but the "main course" couple led more of a parent/child relationship. And most children are not resourceful enough to be able to cope with being left suddenly on their own.

15

Is there a solution? I think so. If you don't have mutual goals that keep you together, common interests to enjoy, and carefully delineated plans for spending time together, you can't preserve the interaction between the two of you. In my opinion, few men care what the baby's new word is after *daddy*. They're not interested in the virtues of one fabric softener over another, or in what your mother had to say during that day's phone call—except in a cursory fashion. A routine life at home gives rise to little stimulating conversation at the end of the day. While *his* life may involve days at a routine job, there is always some little incident that is going to change it. A husband of a full-time housewife can usually predict what will happen when he walks through the door at night. Too often, he doesn't find it interesting and tunes it out.

This is not intended to diminish the value of full-time motherhood. Nor do I suggest that a woman not be available during the early years of her child's life. Those years can be inspirational and exciting because a woman is guiding, cultivating, and developing another human being's personality. At that time, motherhood can be remarkable and fascinating because a child changes so rapidly over a short period of time. However, it's crucial that you marry a man who shares in the child rearing and that there be more participation in the division of labor and less dependence on fixed marital roles. Once you establish a division of roles—women's work and men's work—a man will see the distinction straight down the line. This will distance you from him emotionally and in every practical matter. It means you hear yourself saying, "When I watch the kids, it's child care. When you watch the kids, it's baby-sitting." Or "If I get a job, I'm not a good wife and mother, and I'm pulling the family apart. When you have a job, it's your God-given right."

I was recently talking to a man who holds a glamorous job and whose wife doesn't work. I asked him, out of curiosity, how his wife feels about his life. "She's ruthlessly jealous," he replied with a smile. Then it faded as he continued, "I walk into the house and she can't go for my throat fast enough. She may love me, but she hates me so much, too. I don't quite understand it."

I understand it. It's unbearable for her to know that he's surrounded all day by people who make the world run. It's painful for her to think that he can't wait to get to his job in the morning. It saddens her that he thinks about his job all the time. And why does he? His job is the essence of his vitality.

Where does your vitality come from? How much satisfaction can you really get out of your kids before they leave to start their own lives? There's much satisfaction when they're young and need you, but then what? How often can you tidy up and find busywork to feel needed? The meal that took you hours to prepare is consumed in ten minutes, and there's little to say after that. Where is the rest of your life going to take place?

I once went to a women's luncheon at which an especially unappetizing beef stew was served. To my surprise, the women called the chef out from the kitchen and gave him a standing ovation for this culinary disaster. How many housewives would be applauded for serving a beef stew—and a poorly cooked one at that? In some ways, we appreciate nonsense from men and praise them for the very things we find inexcusable in ourselves and in other women. Yet we

17

"go with the flow" by exalting a man and by diminishing ourselves.

Part of the problem is that many of us have built marriages upon romantic illusions. At one time, marriage was typically entered into for economic reasons, for political favors, or for purposes of uniting families and tribes. The marrying couple had a more practical view of life then. It was two against the world, working side by side. The couple found its niche where there was often security, stability, and sanctuary. As soon as marriage became a relationship in which each person sought personal happiness through romantic gratification rather than a relationship in which both partners worked as a team for mutual satisfaction, the divorce rate skyrocketed.

Let us examine what happens when romance enthralls us.

COURTSHIP AND THE ROMANCE TRAP

Romance may not necessarily have anything to do with love, but it certainly looks and sounds as though it does. What is romance? It is marked, most notably, by a temporary detachment from ordinary life. It is a couple's indulgence in illusions about each other, and even an ennobling of each other. Romance demands a partial distancing from the immediate environment and a focusing on atmospheric conditions that stir romantic feelings and sexual tension—wine, flowers, mutually penetrating looks, flattery, dim lights, and, in the background, violin music straining to a crescendo. Romance is love notes and gifts, and—not least of all—tempestuous arguments that are usually resolved by prolonged lovemaking. It is built on promises to have, to hold, and—one hopes—to keep.

If you are a woman who has been courted romantically, you might have perceived all this heady stuff as an indication that you were loved. Romance was wonderful then. He was wonderful. You felt wonderful. What more did you want?

A happy ending! The happy ending is an integral part of the romantic interlude. And if the man's intention in his romantic pursuit of you is marriage rather than seduction, then you believe you've reached your ultimate goal—the loving arms of a man who cherishes your worth enough to make you his wife.

Many early feminists pointed out that historically romance was the only endeavor from which a woman could derive a sense of achievement. We know this is no longer completely true, given the force women have begun to exert in the business world, yet many of us still cling to the romantic dream. We seek unending passion, rescue by a heroic lover, and a life characterized by steamy looks and devoted attention. And if your "prince" wanted you to abdicate to him, then you did. Is this love? Definitely not! It is romance in its most insidious guise.

Romance is a lovely diversion for a weekend, a honeymoon, a Thursday afternoon tryst, or as a momentary expression of affection on a special occasion, but *it's not a way of life*. If it were, humanity would have stopped functioning somewhere around the invention of the loincloth. Sustain yourself on romance, and you'll starve while sacrificing the pursuit of dinner, shelter, knowledge, and personal goals for that daily shot of ecstasy. The result? You'll both perish, too tied up in each other's limbs to summon the energy for basic survival or the time to experience personal growth.

Searching for the romantic ideal can turn into a wildly unhealthy practice, especially when we confuse that search with the goal of finding love. While romance has a lot of fantasy going for it, love is grounded in reality. And when people love and care about each other, there is no need for the constant breathlessness that romance is known to inspire. People who really care about each other can maintain that mutual caring without a great deal of gushiness, neediness, or dramatically teary entreaties.

Let's look at the difference between the language of romance and love.

The romantic says: "I couldn't bear it if you didn't love me. Tell me you love me again." The loving person says: "I love the fact that you're alive. It does something important to my life, knowing you're in this world and that you care about me."

The romantic: "You're everything to me. Am I everything to you?" The loving person: "I'm happy being with you."

The romantic: "You never loved me! If you leave me, you'll be sorry!" The loving person: "Let's talk about what's gone wrong with us. I don't want this relationship to end."

You can see how the vocabulary of romance has a touch of madness and desperation to it. Fulfillment must be instantaneous, the romantic says, or else it's a sign that the other person doesn't care. Remember, romance relies on just enough illusion to trick you into believing that the way

you both were during a romantic interlude will be an indication of how you will always be—perfect, well dressed, desirable, thrilled at each other's touch, and flawless. Of course,
this is not possible to sustain.

Whether you like it or not, you must get on with your real
life. If it's love you're after, lessen your demands on romance
and take a good, objective look at who's doing the romanc-
ing. Know that love requires real people who can be there to
support each other through disheartening periods—grief,
upsets, financial setbacks—and to share the joy from tri-
umphs great and small.

In his book *Intimate Friendships,* James Ramey says
that the only obligation you have to another person is not to
leave that person in worse condition than that in which you
found him or her—to ensure that the other person is not diminished by having known you. The most that one person
can do for another is not to expect him or her to be the fulfillment of all life has to give. Most mothers have trained their
sons not to seek romance as the ultimate expression and
demonstration of love and the good life. But women are vet-
erans of the Romance Wars—and we go into battle with
each succeeding generation, not learning to fight for what's
best for us, but for magic. If you choose a man on the basis
of romance, idealism, salvation, or "chemistry," the result
will almost always be eventual bitterness and hurt.

In the early stages of courtship, romance is dazzling.
When you think you're falling in love, your vision blurs and
you develop selective hearing. To your slightly malfunction-
ing senses, reality is distorted. You see what you want to see
and hear what you need to hear. What happens? You miss

21

the clues that are laid out before you. A man reveals himself very early in the relationship, and you need all your faculties to be attuned to him.

Listen to the following three "romance addicts" and note in each case the contradiction between the first statement and the second:

"He used to say I was the only woman who could draw him out and he'd feel safe. Now that we're married, he barely speaks to me. I can't ask him a simple question without his jumping on me to mind my own business." The reality: He was always a man who had a problem with communication. She thought she'd changed him.

"He couldn't get enough of me before we married. Now my husband treats me like a piece of furniture." The reality: He was possessive of her before they married, and she adored it. Now she *is* a possession, which was his very view of her from the beginning, and she resents it.

"He used to make jokes about people who wanted to be 'big shots' in this world. I thought he was always funny. Now he's always screwing up at work and says all bosses are bastards." The reality: He never had any confidence in himself, but she chalked it up to his being an "ordinary Joe." She knows now that he's a "blamer" who has serious problems about accepting his limitations and taking responsibilities.

When the veil of romance drops from your eyes, the man you are looking at will be in sharp focus. By seeing clearly, you can evaluate him not by what he says ("I can't live without you") but by how he *behaves* (he sees other women while insisting all the while that you're his only true love).

Some women have told me that their husbands, while beating them, are shouting, "I love you! Don't leave me!"

How is it that these women can stay with such men? The answer is that they ignore their husbands' brutal *acts* while clinging desperately to their *words*—their spoken expressions of love and need.

Nell, a Chicago working wife, told me that her marriage of one year was not faring well. I asked what her husband had been like during courtship. Great! she said. Fun! Generous! But there was one problem. He had tended to drink whenever the conversation turned to more intimate matters. Eventually an argument would erupt and diminish the seriousness of what she wanted to discuss: marriage. Frightened of commitment, he'd drink and become irrational and offensive. Wanting him to marry her, she had excused his ploys to put off the discussion. She had pressed for marriage and eventually got her way.

Her husband didn't change. He still wanted to avoid all serious conversations, didn't want to deal with issues that addressed themselves to marital obligations, and still drank to divert her attention from what she needed from him. "What do you want from me?" this husband was known to say frequently. "I married you, didn't I?"

Nell never considered that maybe she shouldn't have married this man. His diversionary tactics were valuable pieces of information that she chose to disregard. Marriage would bring them closer, she had hoped, but it couldn't. Not when this man believed the best he could give her was his name in marriage.

If you think a man is going to treat you in marriage as well as or better than in courtship, you may be sadly mistaken. There are some men who recognize that what they can get away with during courtship will set up the amount of power they'll have in marriage. Who wants power? They do, and often we don't. Power means having to make decisions for and about ourselves, having control of our lives so that we'll be responsible for the consequences. The less power we have, the more submissive and accommodating we're going to be. And often a woman doesn't live her life; she *gives* it rather than risking the loss of a man.

If you're astute, you can watch what a man does, and if it contradicts what he says, point it out to him immediately. Let him know what bothers you. For example, a man who's made a date with you for eight o'clock and turns up at nine without calling must know it's unacceptable behavior. This doesn't mean you should slam the door in his face when he arrives, have a tantrum, or swallow any feeble excuse that's obviously a power play to get you to wait for him. Instead, a person worthy of respect would tell him, "I was worried about you, and it's uncomfortable to sit and wait for you. The role of a woman who waits is not one I wish to relegate to myself. If you can get to a phone the next time you expect to be late, please do so. If you appear an hour late the next time without calling, both of us will know you're deliberately stepping on my toes." Here you are standing up for your rights without punishing him for what he's done.

Should he respond with "I got caught in traffic (or "in a business meeting" or "at a bar with an old friend") and couldn't get to a phone . . . and what's the big deal, anyway? I showed up!" understand right then the sort of man you are speaking to. This kind of outburst is going to happen anytime you stand up for yourself and offer a critique. This man is a piece of coal, not a diamond in the rough.

If his response is "Sorry. I know how annoying it can be to

be kept waiting; I'll call next time I think I'll be late," you know he's someone who is considerate of others.

There's a moral to this story. The man who was late almost every time you were courting will be very late coming home when he's married. The man who humiliated you among friends for your opinions—"Don't listen to Tina. She doesn't know beans about movies"—can be expected to call you a fool in marriage. The man who insists that his wife be "the little woman," from the moment they take their vows, will be threatened by any attempts she makes to improve herself through education or work. "Joanie's not about to show me up by going to college" (or "getting a job"). Where does she get off thinking she's better than me?"

Women often marry men who have treated them shabbily, but then they are quick to forgive such ill treatment. Such women think that being told how to live and how to think is worth the price of giving up their individuality only because they fear being left alone—not a romantic condition at all. Instead of training a man to be a better person—showing him that demonstrating concern or compassion for someone else's feelings is not a weakness—such women capitulate and let him have his way. We suffer when we continue to cultivate objectionable behavior.

By giving in to a man and making him the main course, while counting the ways in which she enriches his life, a woman volunteers herself because she needs to be needed, thereby making herself a critical factor in her mate's survival. Often there's no payoff.

Not only do we accept negative responses, but nonresponses too. Jackie, a Detroit wife, told me that her husband never said a word about how she looked unless he didn't like her dress—a complaint he lodged about once or twice a year. She knew she looked good over the last ten years she'd been married only because he said nothing; therefore, he was telling her she looked good. Why couldn't he compliment her? Because she did not expect him to acknowledge her. His presence in her life, to his mind, was compliment enough; her silence was affirmation.

By accepting a man's negative reactions, we romanticize the "positive" one: "He married me." That is not acknowledgment but fact. How many times have you heard variations of these statements? "I gave you my paycheck, didn't I? So leave me alone." Or "I come home every night. Do I have to listen to this nagging?"

RULE FOR LIFE NUMBER TWO: *Happiness is what you're willing to settle for, so be careful that you don't settle for the minimum.* From the very outset you must define the limits of what you are willing to tolerate. Don't fall into the romance trap, later to find yourself acceding to a man's fantasies of who you should be. You must understand that you helped to set up the relationship by participating in his fantasies while hoping yours would work out. You're going to get the man you deserve because you get what you ask for. And if you're unhappy, scrutinize your position in his life and see where it went wrong from the beginning.

The more romantic you are, the less real satisfaction your life will contain. Steeped in the romantic dream, you're a somebody. But as you get on with the business of living, the demands of marriage, and the responsibilities of child rearing, you may well lose that status and become, in your eyes, a nobody.

FROM SOMEBODY TO NOBODY

Ruth, a New York woman married two years, suspected that her husband was playing around, but she didn't know whom to talk to about it. She was afraid that if she mentioned her suspicion to friends or family, and she was wrong, these people would believe she didn't "deserve" a man. If she was right, they'd talk about her husband's infidelity among themselves and think she was deficient as a woman—a nobody.

Ruth is typical of many women who look into a mirror and see a reflection of how they look, not who they are. Brought up to believe that getting a man is the ticket to becoming a complete person, Ruth cannot bring herself to believe that *not* having one won't strip her of her right to life. Said one woman, with pathetic conviction—a woman much like Ruth—"If I can't get a man to take me to dinner, I deserve to starve."

Who are the women who think of themselves as nobodies? How does a nobody behave?

A nobody is unable or afraid to say anything positive about herself: "I passed my driver's test. I wonder if they made a mistake." Nor can she describe herself except in vague or general terms: "I guess I like to cook." A somebody would say: "I did it! I got my license!" "I'm a good cook."

A nobody cannot list her strengths: "I don't know if I have any strengths." A somebody would say: "There are four qualities I know to be true about myself. I'm a good listener and a great friend. I'm reliable and I don't give away secrets."

A nobody advertises to others that she's needy for approval and would be willing to do anything to maintain a relationship: "I brought your car to the garage. Do you want me to pick it up for you when it's ready?" "It doesn't matter that you forgot my birthday. I want to forget how old I am, anyway." A somebody is aware of the difference between doing a favor for someone she cares about and enslaving herself to another's directives and approval. A somebody says: "I brought your car to the garage. They'll call you when it's ready." A somebody doesn't apologize for others' intended slights or oversights and would say: "You forgot my birthday and I'm a little hurt about it."

A nobody believes that because she's a woman, any and every man is superior to her. She subscribes to the fixed rules about what the sexes are "supposed" to be and do. These very narrow boundaries keep her in a subordinate position: "Men are supposed to be the strong ones. Women should always do what their husbands want." Living under her husband's thumb, she diminishes the contributions she makes to the household and feels guilty if she wants more from life: "Why should I complain? I'm grateful I have a husband at all." A somebody recognizes that being a woman doesn't automatically label her as inferior. Nor does she feel that a man is doing her an inestimable favor by marrying her. She can say: "My husband has his strengths and I have mine. We are able to survive better because of that interdependence." "My husband is not always right and neither am I. Both of us, though, are willing to hear each other's side."

A nobody doesn't trust her judgments, values, or grasp of the facts. She gives over the authority to someone else: "I think there's something sneaky about Larry, but if you say he's honest, I guess he is." "I could have sworn that Egypt is in Africa, but if you say it's not, I must be mixing it up with another country." The nobody not only surrenders her position on judgments or information; more importantly, she hides the truth about her feelings. She never believes that what she's experiencing is true at all and is content with the alibis that others provide: "I thought you didn't like me anymore. But now that I know a friend from the office is going through a crisis and needs someone to talk to, night after night, I understand." A somebody has faith in her judgments and summons respect from others. She says: "There's something sneaky about Larry's manner. I'd certainly check on him before committing myself to a deal." "Egypt *is* in Africa." "Because your friend's got a problem doesn't mean you should ignore me for days at a time. Tell me what's going on."

A nobody dislikes her own company and cannot entertain herself easily, have a laugh on her own, or go to a movie or dinner without someone at her side. Others validate her existence: "People will wonder what's wrong with me if I go out alone." "It's no fun going places alone—and it's scary, too." "I hate being alone—the house echoes." A somebody knows that if she doesn't like being in her own presence, *why should someone else?* A somebody likes the respite that being alone provides and she is able to bring more of her real self to another—not less. She says: "I won't miss out on a one-time-only showing of *Gone With the Wind* because no one else can go." "I like exploring the city by myself."

A nobody makes no demands—sexually, emotionally, or financially. Fearful that she'll be totally rejected if she asks for gratification of any sort, the nobody becomes accustomed to collecting the crumbs that others throw her: "My husband would be furious if I asked him to make love in a different way." "He laughs at me when I start crying. I guess he's right—I am stupid for starting an argument." "I'm praying for a raise this December. I could sure use the money." A somebody knows that she has the right to ask for what she thinks she deserves. She is willing to take a chance and ask, rather than be taken advantage of or taken for granted. The somebody says: "Let's try something different tonight." "Your insult hurt me deeply and laughing at me hurts even more." "I do an excellent job here; I've brought in two new accounts in the last three months. I want a forty-dollar raise."

The nobody can't say no to anyone. She is always at another's beck and call, fearful that if she doesn't say yes, she will be punished by a withdrawal of love: "Well, I am terribly tied up now, Mom, but if you want to talk, okay." "It's no trouble driving an extra fifty miles to pick you up. I know you don't want to ruin your dress in a dusty train before the wedding." "You're right. Maybe I *will* like this wrestling match better than the last one." A somebody sees the difference between asserting herself and subjugating herself to another. A somebody says: "I'm very busy now, Mom. I'll call you back in an hour." "Sorry, I won't be able to pick you up and take you to the wedding." "I don't like wrestling matches and probably never will. Why don't you go with a friend, or let's decide on something we both like."

A nobody can't be selective or turn anything down. A nobody is thrilled that she's had an offer at all. However, her internal dialog may contradict what she's saying. "Yes, I'd love to marry you." ("He's better than no one.") "Yes, I'll take the job." ("So it's less than what I wanted, but I can't afford to be choosy.") "Okay, we can cancel the evening with the Smiths." ("So it's another Saturday night in front of the TV, but at least he's not out in some bar by himself.") A somebody knows what she wants and can identify her goals. She doesn't jump into situations believing that whatever offer she gets will be the last. She says: "I love you in my way, but I can't marry you. We're better for each other as friends." "Thank you, but this is not the job for me." "If you'd rather stay home, okay. I might just go out for a few hours anyway."

Nobodies don't expect to matter, and they set up situations so they are proved right. A nobody makes a decision because she doesn't think she deserves any more. A nobody will often select a man who mistreats her, because, she thinks, that man sees to the core of her soul and recognizes her lack of worth. And how smart of him! A man who would treat her well is a man who, in her estimation, doesn't have any sense at all!

A nobody has illusions that a man with a lot of confidence can fill that void in her—and he'll have enough in store for the two of them. With a sigh of relief, the nobody murmurs, "Well, he's got it all. I don't have to worry about that now." Often her illusion continues, "If he's around, no one will notice that I don't have much confidence or that I'm scared of life."

Instead of learning about confidence from a man and emulating this quality, the woman who thinks she's a nobody tends to draw inward. Why? Because such women need to look up to a man. Desperate not to be an equal partner, but to make the man the main course, the nobody can shrink to virtually nothing. But it's worth the price, the nobody says, because I can look up to him.

31

One of the truths we have to live with is that we may wind up alone because of death, divorce, or desertion. We have to prepare for it. If you can't prepare for it within the marriage, how will you face it if it should crop up? And if you live as a nobody, where will you be? Every woman has a responsibility to make herself economically and emotionally independent before she chooses a mate, or she will be a "child bride" for the rest of her life. One reason she will not grow is that she has relinquished all her options and let her husband direct her life. But the more you do for yourself, the more you become a "somebody" for yourself and other people. As you become autonomous, you can give up being a nobody—inside or outside of marriage. When you experience autonomy, you can invite people into your life because they're not going to be a threat to you. You never have to worry that you'll become permanently attached to a man as if you were a living appendage.

GETTING BACK TO BEING SOMEBODY

The marriages that work best are those in which two people are attracted to each other, perceive the reasons for the attraction, and then work steadily to keep those elements in the relationship. They are not fused into one being but are two developed individuals. The worst thing that can befall any marriage is both partners deciding to become one. Know who both of you are and you can maintain a separateness, while still being able to check each other if you should start drifting over the lines into a vague oneness. If there's an absolute division of roles and a living out of the idea of oneness, paradoxically, one of you becomes less to the other, not more. Simple mathematics says it all: If two of you decide to become one, that means someone's got to lose an identity.

The goals of matrimony have to be reexamined and the "oneness" falsehood tossed out when the wedding invitations are sent. What do you want from marriage? To share your life with someone you care about deeply, or to be taken care of like a child? To develop common goals with someone you respect, or to marry the man who you believe will reach goals for you? To develop as an adult within an intimate relationship, or to remain a child who must still follow someone else's rules and be judged by someone else's standards? Look at the process and content of marriage, not the longevity. You can be married for twenty-five years and still be miserable, lonely, alienated. Does it really matter that you were married for five years and the marriage ended, but only three of those years were good? Was your goal simply to *get married* because it was expected of you?

The wisest move you can make is to start to become an individual. And you don't even have to deal with issues of the past; these only complicate matters. History is written and you can't undo it, but you can attempt to change for tomorrow by making a small effort.

RULE FOR LIFE NUMBER THREE: *If you can change your behavior, you will change the way you think.* Think too much about what you are doing, and you may become embroiled in old self-doubts that will stop you from acting. You can't go back twenty years and remake your marriage. If you want to improve your relationship with your husband, let go of the old habits and ideologies that kept you constricted.

You can't make disappear what happened over those two decades, but neither should both of you spend the next twenty years accusing your mate of failing you.

Many women have made a commitment to a marriage, and although it may not have turned out to be a model of holy wedlock, they are in it still. For those women who foreclosed their options by effecting this commitment, getting out—if that's what they want—isn't easy. Others may feel regret for getting the man they deserve, yet they hope that all is not lost. For any woman who wants to take some risks, give herself some options outside the home, and realign her marriage, there are methods to improve both the relationship and herself.

How? Start today. Take small steps toward a well-defined goal—one that will give you some financial independence and a chance to develop your skills. Have faith in yourself and make the rules. Don't listen to others who try to dissuade you. Stand up to pressure with all your will. To do that, you need one person who can be there for you. Most of us can't jump into the world alone. It's better if your husband is behind you, but if he refuses because he doesn't approve of your stab at independence, find one good friend who'll help you through and cheer you on, no matter what.

And your husband? Here's a technique that sounds far from profound, but works: Start by exchanging kind words with each other. That's it. Promise yourself that when you wake in the morning, you will make a voluntary commitment to stay in your marriage for that day, and start to create an atmosphere of harmony. Begin with one compliment to your husband, even if it's "I like your smile." He may not respond in kind by complimenting you, but that's okay. Keep at it. Eventually he will come around. It may take the next ten years to redo your marriage; it won't happen overnight. And don't look to him to change it if you've made him the main course. He's not about to relinquish his position of power without a fight.

If, over a period of time, he does not agree that your marriage is an equal partnership, if he can't endure compliments or the intimacy you will be asking for, then perhaps *you* will have to judge which way you are better off—with him or without him. But when you have acquired a measure of self-esteem, it will be easier to leave, easier to state calmly that you don't need incompatibility as a way of married life or that you don't need to assume the role of a nobody so he can be somebody.

I understand the trade-offs in marriage, how we make men the main course, because I did it myself. I met a boy when I was fourteen years old, and decided he was the man I would marry. When he went off to college, I wrote to him every day for four years, reminding him of all the ways he needed me. I was suffocatingly there—even at a distance of 1,500 miles. Eventually he had two choices: either disappear from this planet or marry me. He married me.

He got through medical school with me acting as coach, working at a job, and caring for a small child. Now I see that in the early days of our twenty-five-year marriage, we never gave each other a chance to grow. Only with this tie to him did I feel complete enough to go on. He, in turn, was so afraid to hurt me that he couldn't deal with my dependency. Fortunately for me, his work created some distance between us and I was forced to grow. Obviously it wasn't so great a disaster for me, because I *did* go on.

I never set out to get a Ph.D. It was only a possibility. Here I was working, then raising two children, helping my husband in his career. I thought I'd never make it. A degree was too ambitious a goal. I took courses, but not with the stated design of acquiring a degree. I played it down because it was alarming my mother: "Forget about school. Are you feeding your husband? Who's watching the kids?" And I wasn't clear about my husband's opinion: "Taking another course?" But, miracle of miracles, I reached my goal.

If you're reading this book and you're already married, know that it will be difficult to break with the past and its established patterns, but it can be done. If you're reading this book and you're not married, understand what a marital commitment will mean if you do not consider yourself worthy of a good man and of fulfilling yourself as an individual. There is an attempt, in the scheme of this book, to change your thinking, to help you see yourself as the main course and men as "just desserts." You can't survive on a daily menu of desserts; recall the effects on you. But how wonderfully freeing it is to approach dessert and select one when you're fulfilled emotionally and financially. Having control over your life is as sweet as your reward—a man.

Chapter Two

Receiving
the Message

My father never actually said it, but I knew from the time I was a little girl that I'd better be prepared to take care of myself.
—Barbara Walters, in an interview

[My Aunt Lou] assumed there would be suitors clamoring at my heels, she didn't even acknowledge the possibility that no one would ask me. My mother's version was that nobody who looked like me could ever accomplish anything....
—Margaret Atwood, Lady Oracle

Whether we are bound to old conventions in marriage or firmly entrenched in the New Womanhood, Mother's litany of "words to live by" rings in our ears:

- Give in and don't get a man mad.
- If you make waves, you drown.
- Stay together and avoid disgrace.
- He's the captain of your ship; swab the decks with a smile.
- Marry a nobody and make somebody out of him.
- Be sure your opinions are his.
- You're only as good as you look.

• No one said you have to have a happy marriage. It could be worse—you could be single.

Some of these messages are lived out with grievous results: A forty-two-year-old woman in Detroit tells me of a shattering phone call from her husband's secretary. "I'm having an affair with your husband," the secretary says boldly, "and there's nothing you can do about it but let him go." Though terrified that he will leave her, she persists in excusing him. Why? "Because it's reasonable for him to say yes to a younger woman who finds him desirable," and there exists "no pressure for a man to assume responsibilities for his family." Society is full of temptations, she goes on, "and he's really not at fault. If anyone's at fault, it's his secretary." I ask if he's been unfaithful before this incident. She hesitates, then admits to knowing of two other women. Why won't she leave him, then? She loves him, she cries, and *is* nothing and *has* nothing without him. The message: *All men cheat. Be grateful you're married.*

A woman in New York who earns five times her father's salary enters a third marriage—the second such union with a ne'er-do-well. She's judged the men in her family, and those she's known intimately, and has concluded that few men are emotionally stable or reliable. Therefore, she's quick to tell you, men need her strength and courage to help them become whole and productive. Maybe she gave up a little too soon in the past, but if she just hangs in there long enough, she can rehabilitate this husband. The message: *All men are weak and ineffectual like your father.*

"Don't take your clothes with you," a Kansas mother tells her twenty-five-year-old daughter who is about to get married. "He'll be returning you." Swallowing her self-doubt, the daughter laughs nervously and insists her mother is undermining her out of love, as a form of protection. If she's not happy, her mother must be implying, she'll always have a home to come back to. The jibe couldn't mean that once her new husband got to know her, he wouldn't want to know her for very long . . . or could it? The message: *Who'd want you?*

A young divorced mother in a Chicago suburb decides life is meaningless when her boyfriend of one month leaves her. She felt alive and cared for when he was with her. Without him, she's lost and valueless, she thinks. She perceives her two young children as noisy intrusions who give her little joy and make demands she can't meet. Three days after her boyfriend goes, she washes down a handful of pills with a half-pint of Scotch. She survives her suicide attempt and regrets it. The message: *If you can't keep a man, you're nothing.*

The messages that are supposed to exemplify womanhood, it would appear, give very few of us a complete sense of self without a man. And no woman, however impressive her worldly position, is quite immune. Erica Abeel says in her book *I'll Call You Tomorrow and Other Lies Between Men and Women* that the definition of woman is in transition, while that of men is standing still. Yet with all the social changes meant to benefit women—the easier access to power, the experimentation, the support groups, and the new "sensitive" man—women, for the most part, are stuck living out messages from the past.

The fact is that many of the messages Mother told us are so deeply ingrained that we are often unaware of carrying them out at all; others are easy to spot with a minimum of self-awareness.

Whatever we may want to believe about ourselves, under certain conditions we revert to childlike responses. We're assertive with the butcher, but we cower before the man we love. We accommodate ourselves to others' demands, but we don't demand time for ourselves. We devote fifteen years to helping a husband succeed, then spin wildly, bewildered, when he leaves us for a "real woman"—as if we weren't real when we voluntarily supported his efforts toward success.

Men are perplexed too. They claim that women have always received what they believed they wanted, and have accepted these things as their due reward: care, kids, and a continuity of tradition. Men have simply done as men always did, so why all the fuss? A woman was told early in life what she was expected to be: the mere echo of a man. If, through marriage, a man gained control of two lives and a woman was given mastery of none, well, wasn't that what she wanted, and wasn't that why she married in the first place?

Only twenty years ago, the family was not such a fragile unit as it is today. A man knew who washed his socks. How could he not? His own mother delicately bared her knees, reddened from inching across the linoleum that she scrubbed to a blinding shine. This same toiling woman did his laundry. He didn't want quite the same selflessness from his wife; he just asked that she know the location of the bucket and how to operate the squeeze mop without loading guilt on him for doing what she was there to do. If she relinquished her natural inclination to set goals of her own, and channeled her ambition into creating a better life for both of them—that is, into being a resilient support system for him—she was only fulfilling her historical role. If she had to be less so he could be more, so be it.

Natural roles, the women's movement said, were not only questionable but objectionable. Enough of drudgery, enough of unconditional surrender to a man. It is time to challenge the shape of marriage and its emotional cost. Let's put an end to seduction, passivity, and withdrawal to get what we want, and instead use courage and confrontation.

What some women did, as a result, was break that connection with history to rewrite their own versions of women's roles. Others clung to convention and hoped the ripples of liberation wouldn't wash over them. Their husbands, after all, were being "picked off" by "those women" at practically the same rate as their unmarried brothers. "My marriage is a personal welfare system," one traditionalist told me, "and feminists, the ERA, and equal pay are ruining life for every woman. What would the world come to if women were all on their own?"

If living by tradition was a nasty habit, then finding one's identity was a breathtaking experience. The message of what a woman's destiny was supposed to be could very well be "returned to sender"; the feminist was not accepting the charges. Then something happened.

In matters of trade, the tenacious, self-directed woman got her career. She learned how to sell herself, how to crack the mystifying codes of business to become a corporate politician. A less ambitious woman just got a job that kept her content enough to know she could take care of herself or

41

not have to quibble with her husband over the price of a coat for herself or her child. But in matters of self-esteem and love, some of the old messages prevailed.

One professionally successful woman is still her mother's daughter. She can still be reduced to a whimpering child over a man to whom she can't express herself. Picture this scene: Her boyfriend is late—hours late, as usual—and she stares at the phone, waiting for it to ring, then has a neighbor check to see if the doorbell works. At her office, no one is late when she calls a meeting, nor would she excuse tardiness lightly. With this man, though, she denies her impulses to confront him, accepts his feeble alibis when he shows up, and is relieved he's there at all. Her mother's message? *Take a man into your life, and you take abuse. If you want him around, you'd better take it.*

HOW WE GET THE MESSAGE

Typically, mothers don't sit down with their daughters and say, "This is what I want you to know about life." Instead, a lot of scrapbooks are pulled out to show her how she must fit in, as every woman in the family fit in before her. The philosophy of the messages is often delivered piecemeal. And it may take a few snapshots and multiple references to the past and present for a mother's message to be complete. For example, Aunt Betty, you were told, did well for herself, and such a plain woman, too. (But she knew how to take care of a man.) Aunt Marge was the beauty of the family, and look where it got her—a hellish life with that no-good barber.

(He married her for her looks, then never looked at her again.) A daughter may be confused at this point: Does beauty bring a desolate marriage, or, if a woman is merely pleasing to look at, does this work in her favor in catching a good provider?

"But if thou live, remembered not to be," Shakespeare said, "Die single, and thine image dies with thee." Few parents want this fate for their daughters, and begin preparing them for marriage at the toddler stage. The message to get married is always clear, though the goals in that marriage may not be.

A woman begins to date seriously. Her parents question her choice of men along the way: "Does he have a steady job?" "Where are his people from?" "Why are you dating a Catholic (or Presbyterian or Jew)?" Your answers and their reactions may clarify what they have in mind for you. Eventually you piece together a picture of the man you're supposed to wed.

Of course, some parents still bow to family tradition and set down stringent rules for mating: "Marry only within our class (or religion or race)." "Be a lady, don't look cheap, speak in a modulated voice." "No one can hate a woman who wears a navy-blue dress, so don't be too offbeat." "Marry the right man or others will look down on you."

Except for those mothers who deliver messages chiseled in stone, most don't let us know what they truly want from us. Did your mother want a better life for you, or did she want you to duplicate hers? Your mother says she loves your father, so why does she have contempt for men who remind her of him? Her feelings are mixed. A mother in an unsatisfying marriage may never want to see her daughter endure her kind of disappointment. But if her daughter succeeds where she failed—in constructing a basically healthy union—she wonders if she's lost her daughter as an ally. Unhappy, her daughter and she can commiserate about their lots in life. Happy, her daughter has resilience and strength and may soon be calling to give *her* advice on life.

Those women who loved being wives and mothers can raise daughters who love being wives and mothers too. They will feel safe in their choice of husband, having picked out men who are equally conscientious about strong family ties. Those mothers deliver their messages and set an example that doesn't contradict them.

When messages are positive, they are instrumental in deciding one's fate. They emphasize one's worth and the possibilities for growth. Their message is that the best relationships allow comfort as opposed to melodrama; they offer the option of spending time together or of being alone without resentment, to make love or to not make love without a paralyzing fear of rejection. They say: Make an investment in yourself by having interests, a career, a self that functions gracefully inside or outside of the marriage.

Negative messages are powerful warnings that alert us to what we can't do and what we must "endure." They're designed to teach us to live happily ever after with a man, any man—but preferably one without a criminal record—and we'll be taken care of. Many messages are proffered, as if a woman has no choice in the way her life is to be conducted.

Many of the messages we were given were contradictory and served to confuse us. While we were encouraged to grow up and make our own decisions, Mother was also appealing to the child in us to remain dependent on her. These are double messages, containing built-in traps. If we become independent, we're proving that Mother has done her job as a parent. But she then feels hurt, abandoned, useless, or in need of medical care—the old familiar theme: "Be my baby forever, or I'll die!" Messages may vary, but they are usually a way of reminding you that you'll fail without Mother. With practiced cunning, she undermines you. Often she'll imply that she's the only one who knows your worth (or lack of it) or tell you that if you leave her, she'll punish you by not being there if you should stumble. These double messages should sound familiar:

"If you want to marry Bob, do it. But if it doesn't work out, don't come running back to me."

"Why are you taking a job in another state? Couldn't you find a job here?"

"I know you can take care of yourself, but if you get your own apartment, I'll worry. You know my blood pressure."

"What do you mean, you got a twenty-dollar raise? Why not forty?"

"I don't believe you're finally getting married. Put Harry on the phone and let me ask *him* if it's true."

The double message expresses a conflict within the mother; she wants to keep you a child with almost the same force as she wants you to become an adult. She may not even be conscious that she's delivering a double message to serve her purpose—to batter your self-esteem just enough to need her nurturing. Insisting that she wants what's good or right or best for you only baffles you as you try to decipher what she's really saying. For example, let's look at the first double message:

Should you marry Bob? Half of her message is that you have good judgment and have made your choice. (If you want to do it, do it.) In her estimation, Bob is wrong for you, so if you should defy her, she'll withdraw her love and support. (If you don't listen to me and fail, *suffer.*)

A woman once told me that she'd married a man her mother didn't approve of—a young doctor who came from a family she thought too "lower class." After ten years of marriage, the woman separated from her husband and asked her mother to lend her money for a divorce lawyer. The mother replied bitterly, "I told you he might be trouble, and now the only thing you'll get from me is anger."

While the double message, by its very nature, can be destructive to you since you don't know which action to take to win, the direct message is clear. There is nothing to do except carry it out according to Mother's instructions.

There comes a time when you must stop and say, "I don't have to live my life according to someone else's rules." The influence of the family is predominant, but you are not obliged to fulfill someone else's life by sacrificing your own. If the messages aren't wearing well, toss them out. Blaming our parents and husbands for our inability to get what we want is a gloomy and unproductive habit. Even if those who gave the messages or enforced them are dead and gone, their voices are still heard and their words are followed unless they're tuned out.

Here are three of the most influential messages: (1) *A man is a measure of your worth.* (2) *Protect your man from reality.* (3) *Marry the man, then change him.*

Let's examine these messages and the falsehoods they contain, and see what can be done to defuse them.

A MAN IS A MEASURE OF YOUR WORTH

There is an old joke that bears telling here. Two middle-aged women are having lunch. One asks the other how her children are. The woman replies, "My daughter's life is blessed. She sleeps until ten in the morning and has a maid to bring her breakfast in bed and another maid to clean the house. Her husband didn't object when she enrolled the kids in boarding school. He buys her gifts all the time and takes her with him when he goes on business trips. *He knows how to take care of my girl.*"

"And your son?" the other asks.

"He has a nightmare marriage," the woman answers. "My son is married to a woman who lies around in bed until ten in the morning and expects the maid to bring her breakfast in bed. She doesn't lift a finger to clean the house, and demands that my son keep a cleaning woman so she won't get her hands dirty. She's shipped the kids off to boarding school because she doesn't know the first thing about being a good mother. She nags him for things and more things, and forces him to take her on business trips with him. *She's taking my son for all he's worth.*"

No simple message to ignore, this one. We owe a good part of our confusion and guilt about doing for ourselves to this message in its many forms: No man is going to want you if you make something of yourself. You're nobody till somebody loves you. Ambition is not a feminine trait, so be ambitious for *him,* not for yourself. No man wants a woman who earns as much as or more than he does—except a gigolo. Men want women who look great in the kitchen, not behind a desk. Be a teacher, nurse, or secretary; be the copilot, never the pilot. And that's it.

The message is cleverly constructed. We are, in a way, forever stereotyped by how we accommodate ourselves to others' needs, sort the socks, or reach the goal of celebrating a twenty-fifth wedding anniversary. And because it's important to establish a family life that's loving and sustaining, some of these daily rituals do relate to a woman's fulfillment. But they are not everything. Nor should they constitute the main course.

We're nourished by historical traditions and fictions of the ideal mother who approaches her husband as a servant approaches a master. Even Edith Bunker, among the most lovable depictions of virtuous motherhood and supplicating wifeliness ever seen, took her stand against Archie to get a job in a nursing home. Archie's attempt to undermine her stab at independence by insisting that a "dingbat" like her could make no contribution to any job only encouraged Edith to demand an apology while refusing to quit. Her example is worth following.

What bothered Archie troubles many men. A woman who earns her own money, whether she works in a factory or owns one, poses a threat to his role as provider, caretaker, and guide. John Stuart Mill said that men don't only want women to be obedient to them, they want their sentiments as well. It's not enough to be his slave, a woman must be an *adoring* slave.

Who doesn't know of some woman whose parents (or

husband) haven't assaulted her with comments like "Don't be a lawyer, work for one." "Will art school find you a decent husband or just some bum?" "I know what's best for you, and I say you don't need to go to college." We listen and worry about fitting in, being "real women" without expressing that creative, independent core.

The late writer Judith Wax commented in her book *Starting in the Middle* that after having "perfected a lifetime of stalling maneuvers," she began to do what she feared and desperately wanted to do—write. What stopped her from going to the typewriter until the age of forty-two was confusion. We're all bred to believe the happy ending of a love story. The loving couple, after meeting, becoming infatuated, suffering, splitting, and reconciling, is launched into some frothy void of pure bliss. The happy ending—marriage—is really the beginning of life's authentic trials. The disparity between the myth of marriage as a confection and the truth of it as a cooperative partnership becomes all too obvious when a diaper needs changing or a husband is drawing an unemployment check.

Many women work because they have to, and then wonder how their men will react if they should receive a promotion. More than one competent woman has turned down a raise or a chance for advancement because she feared jeopardizing her marriage by exceeding her husband's salary or position. At home, the screws may be tightened on her role as homemaker while she carries the burden alone for achieving for herself. Elaine was such a case.

When she married her dentist husband, Elaine felt that she'd fulfilled herself. Her mother had preached the gospel to her about becoming someone by belonging to the best man she could catch, and she'd bought it, but with reservations. Since she'd married an educated man whose own mother had been a lawyer, she thought there would be few problems when she started graduate school. Not so. Her husband was patronizing. He thought it was an amusing distraction for her to go back to school—busywork, a break from being with the kids all day. As her intention to finish business school and get a degree became apparent, the situation worsened. He demanded that she drop school and stay home to care for him and the children. Her goals, he claimed, were foolish. When she wouldn't relent, he reminded her again of her primary obligations as a wife and mother. She filed for divorce.

Since his arguments were ineffective and he didn't want to split up, he summoned her family for a visit, hoping the family bonds would shake her back to her senses. Aunts and sisters railed at her fiercely. "No man will want a woman in her thirties with three children and a degree," they admonished. Hadn't her own mother been divorced and saddled with her? She capitulated by dropping the divorce suit, but not the degree.

For five years she settled into a marriage of convenience because "it was easier. At least there was a stabilized situation for me and the kids, albeit without emotional involvement with my husband," Elaine said.

What the message really means: If there is one crucial lament about this message, it is that our upbringing stresses our lack of worth. Encouraging girls to have no self-esteem, so that a man can feel powerful by comparison, sabotages us. And if we're nothing, we need someone to make us something. How disheartening to grow up feeling that our worth is evaluated superficially while our talents and abilities count only toward satisfying one aspect of life—marriage.

And why do we marry? Isn't it to share a life and not surrender oneself? Growing toward something that you want to do can make a relationship develop, too. It's not impossible. But it takes teaching a man to appreciate what you can give him by being a total person. The dividends of your autonomy are there for him as well: You can offer him the opportunity not to break his back all his life, because you can earn money as well. You can contribute toward a financial goal and help achieve it. And should he have a mid-life career change, you can be there for support and your family won't have to suffer economically.

The finest thing a woman can offer a man is herself *as an adult,* someone who will hold him as well as be held.

PROTECT YOUR MAN FROM HIMSELF

T. S. Eliot once observed that humans cannot bear very much reality. This has been taken very much to heart by our mothers, but rewritten somewhat to perpetuate a common message: Men need protection from the truth about themselves. Or more simply, men cannot bear reality.

It may have been voiced in other forms that sound familiar to you. "Men are weak," you may have learned, "and can't help themselves." They may be tyrannical, they may sit back and wait for you to adore them and attend to them, but you know a man's tyranny is a symptom of a fragile ego that needs your constant bolstering. Men are unable to admit that they are wrong, no matter how lightweight the issue, "so agree with him or he'll find another woman to tell him he's right." The hardest thing for a man to do is cope with feelings—his, yours, or anyone else's—so heaven forbid that you might confront him with the bad news that he's hurt you. If *he's* been hurt, let him sulk, rage, drink, or pout. And if he abuses you, verbally or physically, "it's one of the sacrifices you have to make for having a man." Keep the family strong and the marriage whole, the message goes, and do what you can, sacrifice yourself, to ensure that he doesn't find out the truth. Suffocate him with kindness, spare him grief, and be sure he doesn't learn about himself, stop needing you—and leave!

"What's the point of telling him that if, when we get time to be together, he somehow has to make urgent calls or fool with the car?" one woman laments about her husband's inattentiveness. "He denies everything and tells me I'm imagining things." Another's plaint, filled with grudging resolution, goes, "After twenty years of marriage, I've finally learned how to live with my husband, if not happily, at least in a state of truce. He's naturally argumentative and volatile. Why make it worse by calling him on some of his problems now?"

It seems that protecting a man from himself, not "calling him on some of his problems," gives him what he wants: a sense that he's right, wise, emotionally stable, too involved in important matters like work to be bothered with incidental issues like relationships; and the exhilarating illusion that he's in control. Protecting a man from understanding who he is leads to disenchantment, insoluble dilemmas, and, in the most extreme cases, the fracturing of a marriage. The worst thing that can be said about helping a man not to help himself is that the woman suffers. And nothing is more futile than spending a lifetime grieving over how "he won't change," and making excuses for him at the same time.

Excuses—it is with these that we try to deal with the confusing patterns of male protection that we've gotten ourselves into—just to keep the marriage afloat. The excuses often become more automatic after a while, triggered by a man's need for protection. It's almost a ritual, in some cases, like the predictable family menu. Chicken every Friday and "Don't bother your father about your failing grades in school. He works too hard and doesn't need to hear about problems at home." Meat loaf on Tuesdays and "How can I tell my husband I want my own set of friends, not just his? But maybe he's right. I don't really have the time for new people in my life."

"What can you do?" asks Tina, a twenty-five-year-old Detroit wife and mother. "If you love a man, you try to do what he wants."

There *is* something you can do. Look at how the message works. Who asks that the message's dictum be carried out—you, your husband, or both of you? Is the message stated or merely implied that you will be his emotional protector? What is the mechanism that moves you to protect a man, even though you claim it makes you unhappy to do so?

Here are some examples of women protecting a man from himself, which illustrate how this serves to leave the woman—not the man—vulnerable.

Laura and Jane have uncannily similar marriages, although their marital profiles are radically different. Laura, at twenty-five, is half Jane's age. Laura lives in a small midwestern town, and Jane in a large southern city. Laura married after one year of college and has never worked for a living; Jane, holding a master's degree in education, teaches languages at a community college near her home. Laura's husband is a trucker; Jane's is a lawyer. Both have children—Laura, three sons; Jane, twin daughters.

Laura is a mixture of adult woman and gawky, confused adolescent. She handles her home and volunteer community work with enormous competence and flair, but her relationship with her husband with deference and repressed anger.

"For the second time in the last year, Tim has taken up with another woman," Laura told me in a quaking but tightly controlled voice. "The first time I found out about it, the woman actually called me to let me know," she explained. "I had no idea what to do, so I went to see my mother. I had to speak to someone."

Laura's mother offered words of advice no woman should take. "When I told my mother about Tim, she laughed and said, 'Oh! Is that all? I thought you wanted to talk about something serious.' How could she not think adultery was serious? 'Every man plays around,' my mother said, 'and it will run its course.' Don't let him know that you know, she told me, because what's to prevent him from walking out and going to her?" A dutiful daughter and an innocent in such matters, Laura complied.

When I asked Laura why she didn't have a talk with her husband to see if there was anything worth saving in the relationship, Laura chose not to discuss it. Instead, she told me that Tim was under tremendous pressure and "needed an outlet." It's not that he wasn't faithful for most of their marriage, because he was, and this phase would "blow over."

"It's not that he's not sensitive to my needs most of the time," she said thoughtfully. "And while I'm sitting here complaining, I'm wondering why I am. It's not so awful. He doesn't beat me. It's not as if he doesn't want anything to do with the kids."

Evidently, Laura found false comfort in living her mother's messages and, in being true to them, came up with some excuse or another to accept Tim's infidelity.

Jane's story is a more dramatic one, a case where the concept of protecting her man was practically foreordained, and therefore a confrontation was out of the question.

At fifty, Jane, an energetic redhead, suddenly became ill and was advised to enter a hospital for exploratory surgery. Over dinner, she mentioned to her husband what the doctor suggested, but assured him that nothing was seriously wrong.

"My mother told me that men don't like being around sick women and certainly don't like to hear a lot of complaints," she said. "Mike was a bit like that. Telling him that something was wrong would scare him unnecessarily. The doctor didn't know what was wrong. Why alarm him?"

It was discovered that Jane had cancer. She underwent a hysterectomy and was not told that she might have to have a second operation to remove her ovaries. "I asked the doctor not to discuss the surgery in my husband's presence. When Mike came to see me, I told him I was fine." Jane explained that she'd rather be told directly of her condition because Mike couldn't handle it if it was serious. "I knew how to communicate with him," she went on, "and didn't want him to worry. When I heard the news—cancer, another operation, radiation therapy—I realized that I was alone, with no one to lean on, no one to be there for me right then. I was frightened to death to tell Mike, because he might reject me, even while I desperately needed him just to keep going. My daughters were married and had their own lives. What would happen to mine?"

What the message really means: Sometimes we have to come to grips with the reasons why we protect men from the truth. We believe that first they'll deny it and then turn the information around and blame us. Second, they won't talk to us at all—punish us with silence for a day, a week, a month—for daring to challenge them. Third, they may decide we're not worth another moment of attention and, instead of coming home late, won't come home at all.

Some of us do admit to the truth, though; we say we're protecting him, but we're really protecting ourselves. We can exercise a discernible amount of control over a man when we treat him as if he were a hopelessly frightened child. We get accustomed to his failings and cooperate in blunting his emotional growth and development.

What stops us? Frankly, many women like Laura and Jane are hesitant to take the chance to help their husbands become full partners in marriage. Stopping a discussion that is crucial to married life because it may upset him, or pretending something doesn't exist to keep him at a distance from the facts, keeps a man in an emotionally childlike position forever. And should you believe that one wrong move will destroy the relationship—that is, telling the truth or confronting him—you're better off without it! Marriage should be a friendship. In a friendship there may be words exchanged that are hurtful or hateful, but that doesn't mean there is no love in the relationship. If you live in fear of *not* protecting your husband, you're only hurting yourself.

MARRY THE MAN, THEN CHANGE HIM

Changing a man is not an uncomplex vocation for a woman to undertake. Her reasons for doing so may be clear to her, and if asked why, she might answer, as one woman did, "You look at a man and see the possibilities and the flaws. Does he want to be somebody? So you evaluate him and decide whether what he's got is worth the energy it will require to make something out of him." Others are less drawn to shaping achievers, and instead are irresistibly drawn to charmers, drinkers, fighters, the emotionally void, the underdogs. "How do I get my husband to stop watching TV and go get a job?" a suburban middle-aged woman married twenty-nine years to a man who hasn't "found himself" wants to know. "I've been supporting the family for fifteen years now and I'm tired of it. It's not fair but he's just not sure of himself. How do I give him confidence?"

It may not be fair, but sadly, it's the deal she made. He promises that he'll shape up and doesn't; she has an opportunity to remind him of his irresponsibility. She may feel agonized over her choice of a husband. She will probably continue her struggle to save him from total dependence by coaxing, cajoling, or even nagging him to change. But she *needs* him the way he is—under her control.

If you seek out a man in need of rehabilitation, you may

well discover that you're in for a bumpy ride. And though I've heard from those who invest their lives in this message that changing a man is inspired by love, you must recognize that it's also an occupation—and a high-risk one at that.

High-risk jobs provide uncertainty and excitement, especially the kind of excitement that holds out the possibility of success. Unfortunately, few women who undertake the job can truly handle success once their creation—the transformed man—is complete. And they are seldom happier knowing that after all their sacrifices, their conspicuous love and support, and the mutual suffering to make him strong, the man may not need her once he's on his feet. What then? Will he leave her? Will he want her? What's her purpose now? It's painful to think about.

"If I only love him enough," she's said to herself with total conviction, "he'll give up drinking (be kind to me . . . be more devoted . . . stop getting sick so often . . . stay at one job long enough so we can feel secure . . . stop brutalizing the kids and me . . . stop hanging around bars instead of staying home evenings . . . stop picking on me in all matters from the way I set the table to the way I make love . . . be less stingy)." "As long as I have you," she remembers him saying—or pleading, "I won't have to do those things."

But he does. How do we get ourselves into this fix? Our biggest mistake comes when we only listen to the first half of the message and make getting married the single most important goal, never mind the character of the man or the worth of the relationship. The second biggest mistake is believing that how a man behaves and how he describes himself are not indications of his true character.

Karen is a prime example. Her weakness is the emotionally remote man. He's unattainable, unattached, and always her undoing. Such men have different styles, but each harbors a terror of intimacy and the remarkable ability to tantalize women like Karen. "The chemistry's there," she says simply. "Don't ask me why or where it comes from."

Karen dated an attorney for six months. For five and a half of them, she knocked herself out to "make him fall in love" with her. What generated her crusade?

One romantic evening he looked deep into her wide brown eyes and said earnestly, "I have nothing to give you." If she were more self-protective, she might have thanked him for the dinner, left his apartment, and said good riddance. Not Karen. "No," she replied, denying his self-appraisal, "you have more to give me than I have to give you." He didn't know his true depths, she thought. Obviously he'd never experienced real love or real trust from a real woman. She would prove him wrong, and he'd magically open up, feel unthreatened by the force of love, and—why not?— marry her.

So the lawyer took what she had to give (endless attention, gifts, sex on demand) until one morning when she called him to confirm a date. "I'm washing the car and can't talk now," he told her curtly and hung up. She called back and he didn't answer. His secretary screened her calls at his office during the next few weeks. Suddenly he could not be reached. Karen never heard from him again.

The classic losers in the game of "Marry the Man, Then Change Him" are the wives of alcoholics, womanizers, gamblers, and brutalizers. These husbands pledge that they'll change; they may even reform for a short period of time, then lapse into the old patterns. Why do wives stay in relationships where they become nurses, therapists, and essentially single parents, since their husbands aren't available physically or emotionally for the children?

The apologies they make for their husbands are not meant merely to excuse them. It's almost a matter of principle to keep the relationship as it is. "He can be very compassionate when he tries." "He loves the kids and me, even though it's hard for him to show it." "It's difficult for my husband to be a man, to be an adult—but I married a human being with faults." "Divorce isn't the only answer. What would he do without me? Where would he go? Who would take care of him?" "He says he'll change for my sake."

What the message really means: There is no way to change anyone unless he feels there is a need to change. Period. You cannot cure with love. If he's got a fatal flaw that disrupts or destroys the quality of the marriage, take a good, hard look at what *you're* getting out of it. When you start rehabilitating a man, you are taking on a task that's best left to therapists or social workers. Many women think they are helping a man to change by setting up rules and guidelines for him to live by, holding the threat of divorce over his head or monitoring his activities. I don't know which is more hurtful—playing love-nurse or, as with one wife I met, actually contributing to her addict husband's inability to change by buying drugs for him to keep him from a life of crime.

What's going on in the mind of a woman who is determined to change a man? His problems, if they're serious, make him *attractive* to her. Part of that attraction—the "chemistry"—is that he's unattainable or desperately needy. He's an underdog, a man frightened of his feelings, a man who, in his own eyes, is degraded. And the man you choose reflects the woman you think you are. To side with the underdog can be a noble cause, but not when it involves sharing your bed with him.

Outsiders may be prompted to sympathize with your lot in life: "Poor Margaret. Ernie treats her like garbage." "Poor Louise. Al never gives her a dime." But what is left unsaid is that *you've* made the choice. It is not uncommon for a woman consciously or unconsciously to believe that she must have a degraded male because he's all she's worth and can handle. Again, by directing a man who's weak, she gains control over someone at last, someone who is less a person than she herself. A woman in this situation must alter her own behavior before she asks any man to change. Remember, a man who needs help will be less likely to leave you, especially if you're his reliable ministering angel. Chances are he's going to stay.

The message to marry a man and then change him is basically a romantic one. We're not trained to love the decent, caring man, but the romantic figure—the tough guy, the hero, the pirate. Change a cad to a caring man, though, and the woman who's responsible may very well yawn in his face, leave him, and go on to be the savior of the next cad to come into the picture. Romantic love thrives on absence, says sociologist Philip Slater, and he's right. Whether a man is not present emotionally or physically, the relationship is seen as tragic, unrequited, self-sacrificing, and dramatic.

If a man wants to change, be there for him in a supportive position. If he needs help, he must be willing to confront his problems and seek professional guidance. Don't cast yourself in the role of the suffering woman, because if you do, neither of you will win.

FOLLOWING THE POSITIVE MESSAGES

As I see it, the only valid message is that we, as women, can basically have anything we want. We encounter problems when we automatically act out the old messages that cause us unhappiness, dissatisfaction, and pain. We *do* have value as human beings. We do not need to provide love-nursing for the ineffectual or seriously troubled man. We are entitled to opinions and to be able to fulfill our lives within a family setting. We can be what we want to be by reprogramming ourselves with positive messages, of which the following are models:

If I want something enough, I will find a way to accomplish it. Perhaps I failed at a task in the past, but that doesn't mean I'm a failure. The negative message: I'm a real screwup. Everyone was right about me, so why try?

I will find time for myself each day to do nothing or to do something. What matters is that I give myself a break from family obligations. The negative message: My life isn't important unless I do for other people. It's selfish to want a little privacy.

If I am upset, I will tell the people who are involved in a direct and rational way. My feelings matter too. The negative message: If I show my true feelings, I'll be guilty about it. I'll just wind up hurting their feelings and they'll tell me I should be grateful that they're in my life at all.

I recall a patient whose mother admonished her that she was not to do anything with her life but be a good wife and daughter. Nora, an only child, was doted on by her mother, especially when Nora fell ill. Her mother would wash her, serve her, fuss over her, and treat her as if she were an infant back in the crib. Even when Nora was married, she returned to her parents' home when she was sick. Ironically, Nora married a man who was kind, loving, and giving, and who encouraged her to pursue her own interests. What happened? One day Nora developed an undiagnosable "disease" that rendered her unable to walk. And back home she went. Now that Nora was immobilized, her mother was thrilled. Her child returned to the crib. Being unable to walk meant that Nora wouldn't have to continue teaching, enroll in graduate school, or participate in marriage. Now her mother could do what she knew how to do: be a mother.

Through therapy, Nora discovered that she needed her mysterious disease to give her mother a purpose in life. As much as she despised being helpless and confined to a wheelchair, some inner force still drove her to develop the symptoms of an incurable malady. Nora finally faced the truth that she didn't have to give her mother a baby to tend throughout her life. Her mother's message was clear at last: If you stand on your own two feet, I'll lose the baby in my arms.

Nora's husband allowed her the opportunity to go into the world and accomplish whatever she chose to. Instead of releasing her from her mother's web of dependency, that freedom panicked her and she lapsed into living out her mother's message.

To say that we're living out the messages because of love is to cloud the issue. Love is often described in terms that sound like the symptoms of a tropical disease, the fierce commitment to a religious vow, or the threat to one's life implicit in hand-to-hand combat: "When I look at him, I can't breathe, can't eat, can't concentrate; I feel like I have a fever."

"It's your duty to make the people who love you happy." "If I don't do as my husband (or mother or father) demands of me, all hell will break loose; they'll kill me if I do it my way."

What is love? Harry Stack Sullivan offered one of the best definitions I have ever read: Love is when the needs and satisfactions of another are as important as one's own. This definition speaks in favor of an equal relationship where one person's needs are not expendable to gratify the other's.

Too many messages are said to originate out of love. A mother may say, "I'm only trying to protect you from the same mistakes I made, so you can't be an actress." Or perhaps a husband will state, "If you loved me, you'd have sex with me whether you liked it or not." But forces other than love may guarantee the enactment. The girl who wants to be an actress may desperately need her mother's approval and be willing to sacrifice her goals to get it. The woman who rejects her husband's advances may in turn fear that he will reject her permanently. If this is love, do you really want any part of it? Where are the sharing, the mutual goals, the respect, the concern for another's comfort and well-being? Not here.

Scrutinize the messages in your life, and list them. Decide whether you are living them out to another's satisfaction or yours. Which messages would you change? Which messages suit you? Which messages prevent you from being who you are? Which messages tell you where to go and how to think and make you angry, fearful, or guilty if you don't carry them out? Sort out the destructive messages and work toward discarding them. Replace them with positive ones that will enrich your life. If you don't discard those messages that make you less than you are, you could well spend the rest of your days betraying yourself, resenting your husband or father, and blaming your mother for what you didn't get in this life.

Begin by learning to care about yourself. Possibly you will have to go through a painful process by not responding as a child would to a parental dictum. Growth is always difficult, but growing into adulthood is worth all the confidence you will gain. Nora, for one, found out that the child within her was guilty about becoming a woman. She spent nearly a year of her life as an invalid to prove to her mother that their bond was indestructible. They will always be mother and daughter; that is an immutable fact. But for her to recover and walk again, Nora had to understand that for her mother to love her, she herself didn't have to be an immature, clinging little girl and avoid an intimate relationship with a man.

As in Nora's case, you too must recognize the messages and stop the automatic responses that keep you from maturing and realizing your own self-sufficiency. And when you stop those responses, you will have to be ready to endure protestations, anger, or threats of love being withdrawn from you. Nora found the courage to develop self-reliance and discovered that her mother didn't perish from the shock, and neither did she. Nor will you.

Chapter Three

Bringing Up Daughters

I have hardly said, "Good morning, Mother," when I hear myself saying, "Mother, good night."
—Emily Dickinson, The Letters of Emily Dickinson

"Much of the bond that holds us to our mothers," Judith Arcana pointed out in *Our Mothers' Daughters,* "is an unspoken recognition of our sameness, the sameness of our lives, that repetition that so many of us fear."

To want that deep and abiding bond with a mother is normal. But more often than not, the "sameness" we fear comes from a compelling force; it is not only our moral obligation but our *destiny* to be cast in her image, and if we reject her example, we chance losing her love.

Until recently, society assumed there was no question about where a woman should find her identity. She didn't have much of a search. She just had to walk into the kitchen and look toward her mother. Sameness, according to the thinking of the time, made a girl into a woman.

Unlike her brothers, a young girl was not expected to be left to her own devices, to improvise and explore the world.

Her world was her mother, and she was her mother's world. If one word could be applied to a girl's future, it was "inevitability"—she would grow up to be a wife and mother. Our mothers—daughters themselves—were victims of this assumption of sameness in their own generation. And if our own mothers were typical, they protected their role fiercely, tending, doting, maneuvering, manipulating, nurturing, loving, and teaching their daughters who they were supposed to be. A mother's life reflected those deeply ingrained messages that linked her to the past—and to her mother—and ensured that what she knew would be passed on to her daughters and her daughters' daughters. Well, then, what *did* she pass on?

"There was a large photograph of my grandmother on my mother's dresser," one woman told me. "I often caught her praying to that picture, asking the ghost of her mother to give her strength, heal the sick among us, and give her peace. She described her mother as an 'angel.' Her greatest disappointment in life was not being thought of as anywhere near as angelic by her children."

"My mother thought of her life of misery as something unavoidable," another reported. "Why? The women in her family were 'cursed.' The curse meant you married a con man, a drinker, a workhorse who played around on the side. My mother wanted more for me, but told me not to expect it."

"My mother seemed forever troubled by her children's observations and desires," a third woman said. "As an example, I was fourteen years old when I told her I wanted to be a doctor. She said, 'Who gave you that idea? Who told you that you could be a doctor?' It was as if, in her mind, I couldn't make a judgment on my own but had to be influenced by others. Much like her."

In *A Different Woman,* Jane Howard, who speaks fondly of her own mother, states that though our mothers' generation meant well, they presented us with a spectrum of life that was "sheltered and narrow. It took us a while to figure that out," she says, "but within that spectrum, we found nuance enough to feed a habit of self-scrutiny which startled our mothers. 'You sure didn't inherit that,' they seemed to be saying, 'from us.' "

As some of our preconceptions began to dissolve, we learned that Mother, with her certain limited vision, did not think well of herself. Unless she was truly content in her role of homemaker, harboring aspirations for herself while imparting a sense of self-worth to her daughters, she told us in hundreds of ways that women were of little value. Where did she get this notion?

She grew up in an era when a woman's creed was chastity, obligation, and enduring hardship—economic or emotional. In her youth, a sexual experience before marriage could "ruin" her, a child out of wedlock destroy her, and a divorce shame her. She was considered a man's property, and her value diminished in proportion to how well she did her job—first as a dutiful daughter to her father, then as an obliging wife and mother. What torment she must have felt! How arduous for her to fear expulsion from a family or community that would condemn her if she wasn't unremittingly *good.* That goodness was part of her dowry, brought with her from her parents' house, where she sought approval, to her husband's house, where she demanded it. And if she wasn't an ace homemaker, didn't commit the rules of etiquette to heart and be a lady, didn't raise virtuous daughters, then who was she?

"Bad mother" were words that could make a woman either tremble or go for her accuser's throat. Call her a shrew, a hypochondriac, a pinch-penny, but don't challenge her purpose in life and tell her she's failed at her rightful—and only—job.

Many mothers withdrew into their isolated world of home, seeking gratification and affirmation from their husbands and children. It was all they had, and they wanted us to have it too "when we grew up." The traditional role didn't, however, appear too tantalizing. Most of us saw and heard our mothers' lack of communication with our fathers. Our mothers desperately needed attention that was never paid them; they dreaded that they were not lovable. We listened to our share of alarming tales of the cruelty of the world and how women must be protected from it. Each day you were an audience to your mother's recitations of what she'd done for you and her demands for worshipful gratitude in return. When you loved her and showed it, it never seemed to be enough. A fight was treason, and to seek comfort from your father was a betrayal. Since she presumed that you and she were identical, almost sharing the same body, you often heard puzzling but laughable comments like "I'm tired. Go to bed" or "I'm not hungry. Why are you eating?" It was her privilege to belittle you and a matter of honor for you to take her side against your father. As much as she yearned for flattery, compliments embarrassed her and she'd inquire suspiciously, "What do you mean, I should always wear this

dress? Are you trying to say that I usually look like a wreck?"
Life with Mother was educational, but as a teacher she didn't know her subject—womanhood—fully. The culture issued strong directives as to what true womanhood must be, and she took the directives as gospel. What were they? She must immerse herself in the relationship with her husband so that his interests and well-being came first; she must gear her life to the ways in which others responded to her, needed her, loved her. Living through other people because her home was the sum of her own worldly experience may rob her of her individuality, but wasn't that simply the way things were?

MOTHER'S EXPECTATIONS

To have one's existence defined by a man or a family is a painful way to live. Definitions like this one lead to immeasurable dissatisfaction. Women who are dissatisfied with their lives, who have negative opinions of their own worth, pass on a tragic view of a woman's lot in life. And while a mother may want her daughter to be a replication of herself, she may also wish for her a different, better life. A daughter, then, can be her salvation. As Signe Hammer states in *Daughters and Mothers,* a mother wants to "be reborn in her daughter into a positive identity."

Destiny, then, needn't be fixed in the stars, but mutable. For a daughter to live out a mother's dream of what she herself might have been, the mother only requires that her child cooperate in the fantasy. As the mother was forced to com-

71

promise in life, so her daughter will be trained to make her own hard bargains. As the mother was denied an education, so her daughter will attend college and achieve. As the mother remained submissive, so her daughter will have courage. As the mother consented to follow all the rules, so her daughter will define her own rules within legal and moral limitations. As the mother never experimented in life, traveled, tested herself, so her daughter will have spirit, a sense of high adventure, *fun.*

"The danger in this kind of fantasizing," Hammer says, "is, of course, that a mother will overidentify with her daughter, living so intensely through her that she places an impossible burden of expectations on her."

Maternal expectations, then, work in two markedly disparate ways. There's the mother who presumes the inevitability of her daughter's role in life, and the mother who presses her daughter on to an endless quest for growth and perfection. Either set of expectations stems from the mother's pronounced lack of self-worth and a blurring of distinctions between herself and her daughter.

The mother who believes in inevitability will tell her daughter not about life's possibilities, but about its futility. She will set herself up in any number of *personae* for her daughter to emulate: sacrificial victim, resigned drudge, sexually abused little girl, saint, jealous rival with her own daughter for the father's attentions, possessor of unnamed diseases, and heavyweight champion at provoking guilt. These statements may sound familiar to you:

"What's the good of wanting more? There *is* no more."

"Cousin Babs never married, and what agony Aunt Jane went through to have her. This is her reward."

"If I hadn't been pregnant with you, I'd never have married your father."

"I walked eight blocks to buy these apples, and you won't even taste one."

"You should be ashamed of yourself for talking back to me like that. I hope your children give you the same heartaches."

"What do you care about sex? I don't understand what all the fuss is about."

"Never let your father see you in a nightgown."

"When I think of you driving on the freeways, I break out in a cold sweat. Do you really need a car?"

"Here's five dollars. Don't tell your father."

Seeing herself as worthless, this mother is locked into the concept of inevitability. In her discontent, how painful it would be to evaluate what she had in life and come up with nothing. Her daughter, though, gives her something to hold on to by emulating her life. Thus she perceives her purpose in life as being fulfilled, approved of, and affirmed.

What such mothers don't perceive is that the legacy they pass on is insidious. Get married, they say, and you'll be happy. But if you examine your parents' marriage, you might be hard-pressed to see the joy they brought each other—except, perhaps, on special occasions like holidays, birthdays, or other family get-togethers. Married and in a troubled situation, a daughter may go to her mother to beseech her to reveal the key to happiness in marriage. Mother's answer may be contradictory to her first injunction: "Grow up. No one said marriage had to be happy. You make the best of it." In the film *Lovers and Other Strangers*, this question is posed to a pair of traditional parents: "Are you happy?"

"No!" they chorus, as if the answer were a foregone conclusion. "Then what do you have together?" is the next question. The father replies, in effect, "We have a lot in common. We've got food. A nice pot roast with little potatoes, a roast chicken . . ." A hearty meal may bring infinite comfort to this incompatible couple, but away from the table, there's trouble.

From those mothers who believe in inevitability, we also learn that men can't be trusted, nor do they wish to give us satisfaction and compassion; they are emotional hindrances with wallets. The man provides food and shelter, and for compensation, women give their bodies and lifeblood. While indicating that men are the masters, such mothers also, says Judith Arcana, "teach us that therefore we cannot be honest and forthright with men, but must manipulate and scheme to make our way; so our mothers demonstrate their contempt for men." More important, Mother needs to form an alliance with her daughter to ensure that Father is placed in an exalted, unapproachable, or feared position: "What your father doesn't know won't hurt him." "Men are animals, but you do your duty and give them sex." "I do everything to please your father and all he does is torture me." "I said you can't have a new pair of shoes, so you'd better not ask your father for the money." "Start praying that I don't tell your father you're sleeping with Tommy."

Often we are held up for comparison to other siblings and made to feel competitive with them for Mother's love. In her eyes, we are all the same, therefore we are not allowed our uniqueness. To keep a daughter under control, she'll use belittlement and the placing of blame: "Your sisters never gave me a minute's trouble. Why can't you be like them?"

"Your sister is pretty, like my side of the family. You look like your father." "Your sister would never have broken my good dish. Stop lying and admit you did it." "Your brother is popular. What's wrong with *you*?" "Your brother only got a B in math. How did *you* get an A?"

Holding fast to the law that women play a secondary role, Mother teaches us not to aspire to any goal greater than catching a man. Since she has little confidence in her ability to care for herself, she imparts her own self-doubt to her daughters. She feels that striving for a goal outside the home is a masculine trait, therefore she has a rationale for building a wall around herself and her daughters to shut out the world. Also, because she needs to know that her life matters, she desperately clings to her daughters to make sure they follow her own life's patterns. Exploration, this mother feels, is dangerous, and outside influences are threatening: "Depend on a man or you're not a woman." "Men like paying for women." "Men don't like smart women. Never contradict them." "Women with careers aren't normal." "How will he feel if you make as much money as he does?" "The only success you need is finding a nice man and having children." "So you didn't get a promotion. You can always get married instead." (This last may be rephrased: "If at first you don't succeed, you'll get used to it later on.")

The mother who looks to her daughter for salvation basically believes the same things as the mother who lives the "inevitable" life. She too lacks self-confidence, but has secretly always wanted to strive for her own betterment. Her daughter, then, will be her replacement and "be somebody." From the beginning, the daughter is put under pressure to be the best and told how she must achieve: "I gave up my career for your father. The same thing will never happen to you." "Of course you want to be an actress. You have my talent and flair." "My mother wouldn't let me go to law school. I'll make sure you do." "Never marry. You'll never find a man who appreciates how bright you are." "If you're not in the top three in your class, you don't get that trip to Europe." "*I* want you to model. What do you mean, you're not interested?" To qualify for her mother's love and approval, the daughter accedes to the mother's demands, fearing anger and reprisals if she doesn't and feeling overwhelming guilt if she fails.

If a mother's strategy is to keep you under her control by fulfilling her in either way, then what happens to you? If you've rebelled against either dictum, you probably have your own stories to tell about the responses. When a mother's purpose is to make you feel responsible for completing her life, then each step you take to challenge her is an affront to her very existence. Hasn't she done the best for you? Why aren't you making her happy? How did she go wrong? What happened in the scheme of things to make you think you were your own person? These questions haunt her.

If you've followed her beliefs and now question their value, you may feel ponderous guilt about wanting to let go of the old rules. If you explain to her your motives for wanting to change ("I don't want to be stuck in the house like you for the rest of my life; it was okay for you, but not for me"), she may retaliate, "My life put food in your mouth and clothes on your back. What makes you think you're any different?" Each time she says, "I spent a fortune on your education and now you turn around and get married," you will feel guilty about disappointing the fantasizing mother by wanting to take a break from a career to raise a family.

Since she views it as your purpose to make her happy by surrendering yourself to her management, she expects a payoff for all her hard work. It may not matter to her that you are being bent out of shape by her manipulations; you are not who you are, in her view, but who she says you will be.

MY BLESSING, MY CURSE

There probably isn't a woman alive who hasn't been described by her mother as her good little girl or the millstone around her neck. Since Mother hasn't really matured, she still thinks in terms of either/or, with no middle ground that allows for a normal demonstration of appropriate or inappropriate behavior. *She's* either good or bad; her daughter is either good or bad. Most of us fall somewhere between, but can recall vivid episodes of being cast in the role of either blessing or curse.

The underlying message is, "Do as I say, or else I won't love you." This exacts an enormous price whether or not we go along with her idea of what makes us acceptable and worth loving. Since the message is first implanted at a very early stage in our development, we may be locked forever into a pattern of wanting to please her.

The most self-defeating aspect of spending one's life trying to please another is that it cheats us of our own growth and satisfaction. But that's not all. The relationship we formed with Mother—the first person we had an emotional link to, the first person we ever wanted to please, the first person we did not want to make anxious or angry—will forever affect our relationships with others, especially with men.

Did Mother tell you that you were no good, spiteful, evil, that you caused her ceaseless pain by your defiance, that you were a tramp and would come to a bad end? Did your mother tell you that you were a perfect child, so obedient, so *tidy,* that when you were five years old she could dress you in white, take you to the playground, and trust that you'd return home in the same pristine condition? Did she tell you that you never spoke unless spoken to, that without you she was nothing?

Countless women were, as children, cast in such either/or roles and are still influenced by them. How? They select friends, lovers, and husbands who treat them as their mothers did. You need only look at the relationships in these women's lives. The "bad" girl will find a man who will deny her happiness, treat her shabbily, and reinforce her feelings of worthlessness. The "good" girl will choose a man who will baby her, prevent her from growing by insisting she's needed by others, and keep her under his domination because she's terrified to make a move that will displease him.

What other effects does the either/or relationship with a mother have on a daughter? Alice was considered the "bad girl" of her family because she never conformed to the family's ideal: "My mother wanted me to need her," Alice said, "but I got a double message—'Need me, but don't expect me to be there when you do.' So, without her realizing what she was doing or acknowledging it, she taught me to be independent. When I was eight years old I asked her to iron a white blouse that I needed for school assembly. She told me that if I wanted a blouse ironed, I would have to learn how to do it myself. Whenever I had a problem, she'd say, 'Figure it out for yourself.' If I needed advice or help with schoolwork, she'd tell me, 'You're smart, figure it out.' If I did something on my own without asking her, she'd say, 'You can't tell Alice anything. She knows it all.'

"Our relationship was primarily characterized by her benign neglect and my figuring it all out. And for some reason I could never understand, I was assigned the role of the 'bad child' from about the age of three. Because I felt she had so little concern for my interests and well-being, I defied her at every turn. The older I got, the easier it was to challenge her. And believing that your mother has minimal love for you, whether it's true or not, forces you to make a decision about your life. Mine was to need no one—my version of independence. She'd also given me huge responsibilities at home, 'to earn my keep.' In her eyes I was contributing to the household, but to me, I was being coached in taking care of myself and not others, for the blessed day when I would move out and be on my own.

"I left my parents' house," Alice continued, "right after graduating from college. For ten years following my move, my mother called to probe why I had left. What had she done? Was I ashamed of her and my father? Was I having affairs with black men? Was I normal? Why wasn't I married, like my sisters? I told her what I thought to be true of our relationship and suggested that she figure it out.

"While I thank her for the gift of teaching me self-sufficiency, of being able to take risks, I know that this developed a paralyzing fear in me of needing anyone, and a serious distrust of any man who said he loved me. Love to me meant strangulation, having whatever joy of life and spirit beaten out of you, being manipulated by guilt, trickery, and illness into bending to someone else's will. When a man mentioned marriage, I panicked. All I could visualize was recreating that same grim family setting that I came from. That is, I would be told what to do and be punished for not doing it.

"I was thirty-six before I resolved the relationship with my mother and accepted her for who she was. I believe that her inability to demonstrate caring and affection openly came from frustration in her own life. The older she gets, the more she tries to be a caring mother—partly, I think, to make peace with herself and partly because she genuinely wants to be included in her children's lives and have the 'big, happy family' that eluded her in the past."

While Alice's behavior was judged "bad" because she was strong-willed and knew what she wanted early in life, Toni was labeled a "bad girl" because of sexual curiosity.

Toni's bad-girl role originated when her mother caught her masturbating when she was about seven years old. "She dragged me to the tub and scrubbed me down, warning me of the dangers of sexual pleasure," Toni recounted. "From then on, I was doomed. My father had left her, and she began taking out her resentment on me—partly, I think, because I resembled him so much, and partly because I had this 'dirty habit.' To her I was the seductress, the whore who'd never amount to anything. All she ever wanted me to do was quit school, get a job, and pay my own way.

"She began drinking heavily, and when I was in the tenth grade I had no choice but to quit school. It was either work or go without food or clothing. I got a job as a waitress. When I was eighteen, I got pregnant by the man who eventually became my husband. Tom wanted me to have an abortion, but I wouldn't. I'd always loved children and wanted this baby very much."

Toni carried small, and few people even knew she was pregnant—including her mother, with whom she still lived. The night she went into labor, Toni said she was sick and asked her mother to call a doctor. "When the doctor arrived at the house," Toni went on, "I told him I was about to deliver and asked him please to tell my mother about my condition. I couldn't seem to do it. He went to tell her, and a moment later she came screaming into my bedroom like a madwoman, saying that this proved how right she was about me. I was 'trash,' and when I left to go to the hospital, I was never to return home. I didn't.

"Then Tom started on me. He demanded that I give the baby up for adoption. If I didn't, he'd deny paternity. I assured him that I didn't want him to take any responsibility. I did, however, take him to court; I wanted to prove paternity for my son's sake. Tom pulled a fast one on me. He brought a few men to court to testify that I was a tramp and had slept with each of them. Luckily I could prove that Tom and I had had a valid relationship, because I'd saved all his love letters and notes. Tom was proved to be the father by the court and made to pay seven dollars a week in child support.

"When my son was three years old, Tom reappeared in my life. Though we had not seen each other in all that time, he called when he learned through mutual friends that I was about to get married. This seemed to inspire him suddenly to make a move. He said he was sorry about the past, wanted me to marry him, and couldn't live without me. I accepted his proposal so my son could know his natural father. Also, I believed I still loved him.

"After being married for a few years, the truth hit me about our relationship. He treated me badly and had called me a tramp and told me I was worthless—mother's very attitude toward me. I had a good job at the time and was getting promotion after promotion. My husband complained about everything I did—nothing was good enough, and neither was I. Work kept me alive. I found a lot of positive reinforcement there. People would tell me I was smart, that I did things well, that I was liked and respected. At home I was told I was nothing, so why was I trying to be something?

"I stayed married for twenty-five years, then recently left Tom. It was a painful decision, and tough for me to do. But it was either him or me."

The "good girl" can get equally as caught up in her mother's web of defining her, and the consequences can be just as harmful. Ella's mother yearned for a perfect child to reflect her ideas of morality, goodness, and adherence to societal rules. Ella had little room to express herself, make her own decisions, or understand what was important for her and what was not.

"I felt that my mother was always looking over her shoulder," Ella said, "and over mine too. She feared not being right and conformed to some divine code of behavior because of 'what people will say' and 'how it will look to the neighbors.' I was the kid who couldn't wear white after Labor Day because it 'wasn't done,' who had to get high marks in school—not necessarily to prove I was bright, but so that I wouldn't be an embarrassment to the family by being dumb.

I was told never to let boys touch me and to remain a virgin until I married. 'Be a good girl,' my mother always would say, 'and run to the store for me.' 'Be a good girl, and don't cause me any heartache.' 'If you were a good girl, you'd visit your grandmother even though you don't want to.'

"I grew up with my mother's voice ringing in my head all the time," she continued. "I was once on a class trip when I was about twelve years old, and had to use the bathroom. My mother always warned me against using public toilets, but I did anyway, fearing all the while that she would discover that I had violated one of her health codes. My mother wanted me to believe she knew all the answers to life's questions, and I would accept what she had to say as law. I could never make a decision on my own without worrying whether I would offend her. I slept with my husband before we married and felt horribly guilty and fearful of what she'd say if she found out. As much as I wanted to be myself, another part of me was totally taken over by my mother's hundred commandments of life.

"I took the easy way out and married a man who would also make my decisions and shame me into carrying out his orders. From him I heard, 'I work my tail off all day, why can't you give me what I want?' By this he meant why didn't I perform in some sexual way for him. When I was a child, being good meant that my mother would love me and not put me in a foster home, as my aunt did with her child. When I married, being good meant my husband would not only love me but respect me. I felt it wasn't true in either case.

"Neither my mother nor my husband cared much for my opinions or feelings. Their feelings and needs came first, and I was there to service them. They decided what was permissible for me and what was not. I somehow lost all respect for myself, and to gain some of it back, I worked even harder at being *good.* I'm still playing out the old rules, but little by little I'm trying not to be the receptacle for everyone's judgments. So far, following my mother's rules have gotten me nowhere."

HOW MOTHERS MAKE MEN THE MAIN COURSE

The consistent message that mothers deliver to their daughters is that they are not complete people—first without Mother, then without a man. One of the commonest ways of communicating the "main course" concept is to tell a woman that she is not decisive and has no authority. Being a female, in Mother's eyes, means never having to take care of oneself. If she had any sense, say the traditionalists, a woman would consider lifetime care a luxury. If you give up a chunk of yourself in return, you've still got enough left over to dream about what might have been. And no one can take that away from you!

Affirm Mother, then affirm men—this is the banquet that all women have been mandated to attend. There are few nods of approval for the woman who won't sample the main course, and a pat on the back for those who relish the loss of selfhood and even go back for a second helping.

What is carefully withheld from a woman is the opportunity to make choices without fearing that she'll be considered less than a woman, a disappointment as a daughter, a failure as a wife. The result? Women eventually grow to dislike, even hate, themselves and to look to men to rescue them and give them what they can't give themselves. But here's the catch. If you don't like yourself, you will question generosity when it's extended to you. The most profound question you'll ask is "Why should anyone be foolish enough to give me, a worthless being, anything of value?" You will even begin to demean the giver, judging him a fool.

If you don't believe you deserve what you're getting—love, attention, material possessions—the relationship will deteriorate. And despite your yearning to gain self-respect and self-love through another, you will be unable to accept any positive messages until you believe in yourself. Remember, if you don't want to be with yourself, why should anyone else?

While dining on the main course, you may complain about the menu, the service, and even the cook. But if you're starving, you will fill your plate—even if it's with a hearty portion of leftovers.

When we are taught to make men the main course, we are also told that what others demand of us is reasonable, but what we want for ourselves is ridiculous; that we shouldn't trust our instincts; that we must remain in menial or low-paying jobs. We feel doubt about our confidence in going out into the world and making it on our own. We are told, as I heard recently from one woman, that a woman gives ninety percent to a marriage and a man gives ten percent.

Is there a way to free yourself from Mother's rules and help yourself? Is there an alternative to dissatisfaction with the inevitable role? Can you make a man "just desserts" without losing him?

BREAKING THE CYCLE

I recall sitting in a group-therapy session with ten women—a few divorcées, others who were single, and all of them trying to cope. They related stories about their mothers and their mothers' concerns over how they would make it without men. Listening to the unspoken side of the conversation, I heard a desperate cry for approval from a fantasized version of their mothers. These fantasy mothers were their mothers as they looked now, but with a few alterations: They'd be all open arms, tenderness, and protectiveness. They'd be rosy-cheeked with excitement at seeing their daughters. On an impulse I asked, "How many here love their mothers?" Nine out of ten hands went up. My next question: "How many of you *like* your mothers? Would you select her as a friend to spend time with, if you had a choice?" One hand went up.

The essence of this impromptu survey revealed that these women agreed to sharing a love-bond with their mothers, but would rather not spend five minutes with them. Was I mad to suggest that they socialize with the women who brought them into the world, that a woman might confide in her mother and expect compassion, comfort, mutual understanding? Enjoy her *company*?

An important part of getting Mother—and her messages—off your back is to acknowledge that she was good enough to allow you to survive. So now ask yourself: *What do you want from her?* Must she approve of you? Must you approve of her, rather than honor her and the values she chooses to live by? When you're an adult, no longer a little girl, you understand that your mother doesn't have to like you and she certainly doesn't have to love you. It sounds harsh, doesn't it? But that's the truth of the matter.

The real question: How do I get her to accept me as an adult? How do I approach her so she respects me and my right to make my own decisions? The more we grapple in the old power struggles over who loves whom, who will get whom to do what, the more we become entangled in the battles we fought with Mother in childhood. For many of us, there is still a little girl within us, yearning for an ideal mother who will give us unconditional love and support, no matter what we do. This is nonsense!

Your mother is a person in her own right, a product of her generation and upbringing. Because we can be more communicative today about our psychological processes, we don't have to use denial or evasion as survival tactics, as she may have done. Look at your mother and realize that you can have compassion for this woman who may have lived only a small part of her life. Of course, there are women who loved their role of wife and mother and who have not created conflicts for their daughters. Being satisfied with her role meant that she had no investment in making you miserable while shaping you into someone you did not choose to be. A mother who felt complete within herself will always recognize that you have the right to create your own life.

In some ways, the worst hindrance to our becoming adults is that we behave like children around our mothers. All of us want to go back home with the fantasy that "this time it will be different." You know the actual scenario, though: a cheerful greeting, two minutes of conversation about the transportation getting there, then—pow!—you're at each other's necks. The fantasy mother doesn't exist, nor can a mother become one merely by wishing it. She will not be beautiful, kind, creative, generous, good-humored, a nondrinker, a ball of fire, a good sport, or a great cook. She won't be able to have a heart-to-heart discussion about sex, nor will she remove the curlers from her hair when others are in her company. Very few of us had ideal mothers, and those of us who did probably had a rough time leaving them.

A good mother does two things: She teaches her daughter to walk, and then to walk away. Walking away is your test of adulthood. Part of taking those steps is to realize that what she says now doesn't make any difference. We'd like to earn their respect, but if they haven't earned ours, it's going to be difficult for us to back away from their influence.

So let's deal with your mother as she is.

First, get in touch with your mother's view of the world. Was it safe? Was it fair? Did she have faith in your judgment? Did she police you? Did you "test her love" by committing self-destructive acts? ("I'll run with a bad crowd and show her." "I'll screw around, and let her try to stop me.") Have you spent so much energy on trying to hurt her that you wound up being hurtful to yourself?

Examine in detail the messages she gave you. Were they unpleasant, or were they just delivered in an unpleasant manner? Was it the weight of her own unhappiness that made them sound unintentionally bitter? Perhaps she wanted you to marry young, realizing that the world was very hard for single women. Maybe she couldn't send you to college, not because she wanted to deny you an education, but because there wasn't enough money. Do you blame your mother for your unhappy marriage? Part of our struggle with Mother and her messages is to realize that we are still tied up with her perceptions of the world and how she wanted us to fit into it. If you're going to change, begin by separating out her messages from her actual intentions.

Next, come to terms with the similarities that exist between you and your mother. Don't censor yourself. "You're just like your mother" is a statement that makes a few million of us shudder. But what is the truth? Do you have her temper, her lack of patience, her attitude toward money? Do you believe that what you want is what you are owed, as she did? Can you be a little kinder to her? What other model of womanhood did you have but her? Even the Medusa-like mother, the worst of the neglectful, abusive, narcissistic mothers, has some good traits. They're worth regarding. What are her positive and negative points that exist within you? Acknowledge them. You will have to list these qualities for your betterment. Why? The qualities that you share are the very ones that will always get you into trouble with her. If you look at what you fight about, it may have less to do with the actual issues than with each of you wanting agreement from the other.

When we empower people as legitimate authority figures who give us messages about who we are, we tend to believe them before ourselves. How many times have you said, "I want to get a job, but my husband says I'll never have the energy to shuffle to the door, never mind making money." Who are you believing if you don't take action? Someone else! Your mother planted that self-doubt long ago. Your husband is reinforcing it. Give yourself the power to take your own road in life, and only ask directions when the guidance is to your advantage.

Finally, take time out to ask important questions about

where you are at this point. Do you feel that the person you look to for approval is yourself, your mother, or your husband? Be honest. This is a crucial question. What was the message your mother gave you about life and your own worth? Did you fulfill that message? Does she like you because you did? Did she change the message at some point? If you rebelled against her messages, whose messages did you live out? Are they working for you?

Examine your life as a whole. Are you satisfied at this time? If you aren't, try to articulate why. What kinds of things would lead to your having more comfort? What are the things you might do to improve your life? What would make you comfortable over a five-year period? What would you like to accomplish, and how do you see yourself getting there?

List five things you like about yourself and five things you don't like. List five traits you'd like to change. Organize them in order of priority. What is the single most important trait you'd like to change? Then work down the list. What can you do to bring about the changes? Do you think you may have to seek professional guidance?

Many of our strengths are transformed into weaknesses by our mothers and our men, who need us to affirm their lives. What are your strengths, your weaknesses? Did you, for example, list crying as a weakness? It is not a weakness to cry unless it's your only means of communication. Openness and vulnerability are weaknesses only when you allow others to walk over you, not when you permit others to see you as you are. Become the judge of your own actions. Be able to say, "I wasn't pushy in that situation. I stood up for my rights." "I wasn't a bitch. I protected myself." "I wasn't asking for a fight. I wanted to hear what he had to say." "I wasn't a lousy daughter. I just did it my way."

Until we ourselves become the mothers we always wanted to have, we will be seeking permission, approval, and love from them for the rest of our lives. If you accept the condition that your mother must love you on your terms while you hate her because she won't, you will always be subordinate to her and powerless to change. Bitter disillusionment in the mother-who-never-was locks you into childish reactions. If you are discontented with your interaction with your mother, what can you do to change the relationship so it works? The answer: Let go of the little girl within you, learn to resist the compelling pull of your mother's emotional force, and cut yourself loose! It may be a painful, frustrating, confusing, and depressing experience at first, but if you see your relationship with her clearly, there is little doubt that you will emerge a confident adult.

Chapter Four

Fathers and Daughters

I wanted to be comforted by your love until the end. In short, I am a man who happens to be your father.
—*Eugene O'Neill,* Strange Interlude

I had always lived not to be my father. Through the years, I had made a portrait of him which I had sought to destroy in myself. On the basis of a few resemblances, one fears total resemblance. I did not want to be him.
—*Anaïs Nin,* The Diary of Anaïs Nin, *Volume One*

A friend of mine grew up with a vivid impression of her father, yet, through force of habit, she referred to *both* of her parents as "my mother." It sounded like this: "My mother is going away for two weeks." "My mother is going to a wedding in Pittsburgh tomorrow." "My mother won't let me go to camp." Though Irene's father was quite alive, we all assumed that the man never accompanied his wife to any social functions and certainly lacked the clout to reverse his wife's decision as to how their daughter would spend the summer. When she married, Irene's vision of the compound parent continued. "We're going to my mother's for Thanksgiving." "My mother bought my son a bike." "My mother is thinking of moving to California." By then, those of us who knew Irene were comfortable enough with her vernacular to inquire whether these situations included her father.

Of course they did.

Why had Irene's parents fused into one being—the mother? How could a man who had made his presence known in the house become a vague figure to his daughter? How had parenthood and all it represented become embodied by a stout blond woman whose voice was the only one Irene heard, acknowledged, or heeded? Who was Irene's father to her, and why is her perception of the "missing" father so common to many women?

When we were children, Mother was the primary love contact to whom we looked for open affection and approval. But Father, typically not available to us with the same ongoing intensity, affirmed his love for us and contributed to our development in equally important but critically different ways. What part does he play in our development?

First, her father is a girl's first male love. His interaction with her will forever affect her sense of worth as a female in regard to any other man. Second, it is her father who teaches her to be assertive—directly or indirectly. A girl will learn, through Father's relationship with Mother, whether women may exercise the right to defend themselves or forever see self-assertion as a male privilege. Finally, since most women do not have mothers who worked *for the love of work*, but out of economic necessity, Father will be instrumental in deciding whether or not his daughter will have a career. It will be Father, then, who will serve as a model for achievement, not Mother.

The interplay of Father's role and Mother's role will either affirm a girl's sense of herself as a woman of worth or set up a number of conflicts within her. Since such a small percentage of women come from homes where there was an ideal balance between father, mother, and daughter, most women, by the tender age of ten, already suffer from a lack of self-esteem in one way or another. We may feel, by then, that not only has Mother failed us but that the evidence is against Father too.

Fathoming our relationship with Father is a lifetime process. We've lived a number of years with an opinion about this "first love"—some of it based on emotion and fact, some of it based on fantasies and assumptions about him. We may admire and fear him—he's the benevolent dictator. We may feel that he's the only man who ever truly loved us, and determine that all other men are deficient by comparison—he's the hero, we're Daddy's girl. We may see him as a dope, a wastrel, the man who never grew up—he's the lovable failure. We may both like and love him, but feel enormous discomfort in his presence because there's never been a solid ground for communication—he's the strong, silent type. We may have found the relationship with him so disturbing that we are unable to discuss him with others—he's the monster. We may have so deep an attachment to him that Mother loomed as a significant force to keep us apart—he's a god. We may love him, but have never told him so. We may despise him, and let him know it in the most indecorous terms. We may have adored him up to a certain age, then never quite forgiven him for being who he is—a man with faults who did not live up to our expectations. We built a pedestal to hold a peanut and felt foolish, or even tricked.

THE EARLY RELATIONSHIP: THE ADORING FATHER

Studies on human sexuality show that a father exerts greater influence on a daughter's consciousness of her own feminity than on a son's consciousness of his own masculinity. How is it that this occurs?

By responding to his daughter as male to female when she is a very young girl, a loving, accepting father will give her confidence that she can attract and interest a man. He enjoys her, delights in her attentions and flirtations, and responds to her gestures of affection without irritation or embarrassment. The ridiculing father, or the father who is absent or is angered by her insistent attempts to charm him, has the reverse effect. Dr. William S. Appleton, in his book *Fathers and Daughters,* says:

"Too little or no childhood closeness to an accepting father can leave a woman with various kinds of scars; insecurity is one of the deepest. Detachment is another because she does not know how to be close to a man and feels cut off. Not frightened necessarily, she simply does not expect love, closeness, warmth, or intimacy from a man."

The first stage of the father-daughter relationship begins when a girl can tell the difference between her parents. The more mobile and verbal she becomes, the more she demonstrates her feelings toward him. If her father is loving and accepting, the ages of one through five will be the most wondrous for her. At that time she's Daddy's perfect little girl—and never again will she find the kind of love and approval from him that she receives from him then. She will entertain him, worship him, insist that his lap is the only comfortable seat in the house. And when Daddy comes home, Mother, whom she also loves dearly, becomes a dragon in skirts. The little girl is Daddy's starlet, and Daddy is the man she wants to marry and have for her own. Mother can take a hike.

When she reaches school age, her world view is broadened. Father is still important to her, but she's no longer his precious little girl. A cooling-off period ensues—but the bond is still one of warmth.

As she goes through adolescence, starts to menstruate, and begins to date, Father will understand that she's on the road to womanhood. Deep inside, he recognizes that he has some conflicting feelings about her emotional and physical growth. Primarily, he doesn't want to lose her to another man, but he knows, realistically, that he must let her go. He does not like to ponder her loss of virginity—and to whom it will go—but he knows that soon enough, a man—a *stranger*—will have exclusive rights to her sexuality. Should Father be a man who has a healthy and emotionally fulfilling relationship with his wife, he may be able, with utmost gentleness, to instruct his daughter as to how she should express her sexuality. That is, he may advise her that sex is fine, but only after marriage, or that sex is fine when experienced with intelligence and discretion before marriage. His own emotional health, integrated with his sexual codes, will dictate his decision.

So far, the loving, accepting father appears as a man who's too good to be true. And he is, until his teen-age daughter beholds him as an earthly being with defects and limitations, not a divine creature who's all giving, all good, and always there. It's this perception of her father as a real man to which a daughter must reconcile herself. This is a painful time for her. Well, here's Daddy now, a cruder and far more disappointing version of the former man. He's drinking too much; doubting his sexual appeal to women other than his wife, perhaps Father takes a mistress or two, or more. His job is a grim reminder that he didn't achieve all he'd set out to, and life, in general, seems to be colored a muddy gray. His wife, older and thickening around the middle, reminds him of his age, and his daughter is fighting her way through the torments of adolescence and has the nerve not to need him as she once did!

Her success in grappling with the reality of her father will be important to the way she will view other men. When she succeeds in accepting her father as basically a good man with good instincts but otherwise flawed in ways she can count, she can free herself of the worshipful and all-forgiving bond with him. By doing so, she will gain a valuable insight: There is always ambivalence in a love relationship, and no one is perfect, herself included. This means she can love a man and dislike him five minutes later; want his company, and then not be able to endure the sound of his voice; know he can be supportive to her at times without her asking for it, and be unconscious of her needs at other times. This is normal human behavior.

Because she has had a healthy relationship with her father, she will then be confident enough to choose a man much like him. This man's similarity to her father will be that he too is capable of normal human behavior. Her father was a friend; therefore her husband will be a man who will not close off her options by discouraging, demeaning, or humiliating her in her efforts to express herself. Her father could be trusted; her husband will be trustworthy. Her father was caring; her husband will be of like mind. Her father had flaws; her husband too will have acceptable frailties.

Many women become stuck in the early stages of the father-daughter interaction. Father may have been excessively attentive, protective, and enthusiastic in his applause. Childhood then becomes hard to surrender. As a result, this woman's self-esteem is dependent on others' approval of her. She desperately needs a man to protect and admire her. Often she will jump a generation and marry a "father figure" who pets and pampers her with the kind of wholehearted devotion she craves. Misery, to her, is being deprived of a loving man's company. It's not unusual for a woman like this one to deceive herself and summon far more practical reasons for marrying him.

Dina, married twice, to men respectively twenty and twenty-eight years older than herself, insists: "Loving an older man has less to do with that paternal feeling than with their experience in life. They always know so much more, have done so much more. That means I learn more from them. Agreed, I do get my way, but probably no more than other women with men closer to their age."

Dina's emotional makeup, and that of women like her, is beset by a number of dilemmas. Criticism from a man hurts her to the quick; after all, Daddy never offended her by pointing out her mistakes. Did she have them at all, she might ask herself, or is this man merely persecuting her? The criticism that most exasperates her is the edict to "grow up" and participate in the marriage or function independently of him. "Why do I have to pay the bills? I didn't have to do that before we were married," she may protest, or, "I don't want to go shopping alone. Before we were married, you always went with me to pick out my clothes."

Since Daddy was unerring in all he did, the little-girl wife cannot cope with her husband's misfired decisions. Should he make a left turn off a highway when he should have gone right, this woman assaults her husband for his ineptitude. Mistakes of any sort are intolerable to her. Because she has an exaggerated sense of her own importance—in reality, evidence that she undervalues her worth—no incident in her life is without disproportionate significance. "I was recently at a garden party," one such woman sniffed, "where there were three hundred people and one bee. Guess who he picked out of the crowd to sting?"

Since this woman, still stuck in early childhood, needs excessive approval, she will become a joiner and a follower. She will note what others do before making her decision to act. She will wear what others wear, have no original thoughts, and never risk expressing her individuality, in case others might shun her for doing so. And her husband will never compare in generosity to her daddy.

Let's backtrack now and see what happens when Daddy's little girl gets stuck at the worshipful stage during adolescence. If Father doesn't fall from his pedestal, she will be emotionally tied to his need for adoration. Much cooperation is needed to perpetrate this *folie à deux*. Verbally or nonverbally, Father will tell his daughter that no man can fill his shoes. What he supplies to her emotionally and financially, says he, will never be duplicated by another man, no matter how estimable his love or vast his generosity. The all-giving, all-clinging father cannot let his daughter go. Why should he? Who else but his daughter adores him consummately?

This emotional tie can result in a woman who will forever seek her father's assistance in life—whether she marries or not. Often she will marry because she believes that removing herself physically from her father's presence will end her struggle with him. Then something happens. Daddy's prophecy that no other can be as good as he is comes true. "I want a fur coat," she demands of her husband. He refuses. Daddy buys one for her with pleasure. She may believe that she needn't give anything to a man but her *presence* to get love. That was the way it was with Father, and her mere presence is all she knows how to give. She may realize that Father has flaws, and manipulate him to get her way. Father is well aware of what she's doing and more than willing to pay the price. She may steal from him or destroy his property—even destroy his marriage—but he will not give her up and allow her to be a grown-up woman. Father knows that as long as his unconditional love does not run dry, his daughter will return to him. And this "daddy's girl," knowing her father will forgive her, no matter what her sins, will forever make her relationship with him the primary one. Her relationship with her husband will be incidental.

THE EARLY YEARS: THE "MISSING" FATHER

When little girls with loving, approving fathers are leaping across carpets in a whirl of childish spectacle for Daddy's eyes only, those deprived of a father—literally or figuratively—are still hugging Mother. If a girl's father has left the fold because of death, divorce, or desertion, she will never again get the chance to test herself vis-à-vis a man. Unless there is a male figure in the family who assumes the father role—an uncle or a grandfather, for example, who relates positively to her—she will be bound to her mother and feel the grave loss of a man.

When her father dies, the young girl feels insurmountable grief and loss. But her mother can reassure the child that his parting had nothing to do with her. His love for her is not irretrievable when she's been told that there was, indeed, love between them. Divorce, though, can be more painful. Father, after all, is still out there. But will his love be available to her? This depends on Mother. When Mother is bitter over the divorce, she could well want her daughter to share her low opinion of the man who has left them.

To guarantee that she is not alone in her misery, the destructive mother could invest her energy in trying to destroy whatever fondness her daughter cherished for her father: "He comes to see you only because he has nothing else to do." "He takes you out because he's guilty, not because he cares to please you." "What makes you think a man like that could care for anyone—even you?" Thus the daughter's self-esteem is battered, her relationship with a parent she wants to love and admire is undermined, and her mother may well be driving a wedge unwittingly between herself and the daughter she wants as an ally.

Many fathers are so work-invested or self-involved that they have little interest in their daughters' needs; they may be physically at home but emotionally live elsewhere. A daughter's efforts to please such a father may be greeted with peremptory disregard or all-out temper: "Sure, it's a nice painting, now go play with your toys." "I told you not to bother me and quiet down!"

It isn't long before rage is the daughter's strongest emotion toward her father. The older she grows, the angrier she gets. And because she sorely lacks that period for testing herself, she never manages to establish a feeling of trust with her father or any man. Dr. Appleton says of this deprivation that many women may exhibit these conflicts with Father by showing no sexual desire for men. "A girl who has not been aroused by her father's attention," he states, "is unlikely to feel strong sexual passions as a woman. She grows into a wife who can perform sexually for her husband, but has no interest in him or anyone else."

Deprived though she may have been of a father, many a woman *will* seek out serial romances or marriages for the thrill of conquest. Daddy may have turned her down, she thinks vengefully, but other men will not. She needs the excitement of a new face, a new body, a new presence. However, enduring relationships are not her strong suit. She will soon find reason enough to leave her man of the moment and go on to another.

Often, a woman who feels deprived and angry in her relationships with men had a mother whose emotions paralleled her own. Because her husband was inaccessible even when he was home, the mother may have used her daughter as a scapegoat for all her own unhappiness. The daughter of such a mother might be told that men are enemies who shelter, clothe, and feed their captives; she might be told that all men are lechers, the sex is a crime against women. And yet, in spite of all this, the mother will urge the daughter to marry as soon as possible! The daughter is put in quite a bind, emotionally disinherited by both parents—ignored by her father and assailed with bitterness by her mother.

"My father made it clear that he wasn't interested in me," one midwestern woman told me, "and my mother made it clear that whatever he did have would be given to her. I had a huge distrust of men, yet desperately needed them to want me—which would prove I was a girl. I had a boyfriend in my senior year in high school, but would never invite him to parties. I dreaded being around other women with him, certain that I'd lose him.

"I married at twenty-two to a man I practically worshiped. I told him I loved him all the time, but he never said he loved me until we were married for almost four years. My marriage was a mess, but I stuck it out. I went into therapy and finally got to see what I needed from him. He was going to be the man who'd save my life—he'd be my lover, husband, friend, and father. I idealized him and couldn't endure his faults. I put him through hell while believing that he was doing the same to me. He was a good, stable, basically loving man, but I wanted a hero—the kind of man he couldn't be and wasn't."

The father-deprived girl who never had Daddy when she was an innocent goes through a stormy adolescence as she begins to experience herself as a growing adult. She's rebellious, defiant, always testing her limits—but still dependent upon her parents for approval. She feels unattractive and undesirable, and doesn't believe she could be otherwise. Her marriage will be a battleground. Since her self-esteem is so low, she struggles for recognition, often pushing her husband to succeed for her so others may see her as worthy. Others set standards for her; she'll judge herself and her marriage in terms of what other women get from their husbands. She seeks to control men: "Janet's husband took her to Paris for their anniversary. How come we only went out to dinner?" Her own husband must provide status, and she will set up a competitive spirit between him and other men in the community: "Ken got a promotion after two years at the company. If he's a manager now, why aren't you?"

When marriage becomes dull for her, she's not averse to the ferment of an extramarital affair. But the lover she chooses may be demanding and indiscreet—the sort who will not hesitate to call her for an intimate chat when he knows her husband is at her elbow. Her marriage may be dull, her lover reckless with her privacy, but this woman needs provocative relationships. And if she doesn't find one through sexual adventure, she will get it at home by instigating trouble.

Other women emotionally bound to remote fathers may go on to successful careers. Thinking they will finally gain recognition from their fathers in a manner that men understand—work—these women become fierce competitors. They may or may not compete with men, but they climb to the top with a vengeance. Getting ahead is the point; it need not be a woman's way to get back at her father by becoming as good as or better than he is. In many ways, the proof of success in a career may be the very thing she requires to help her think through her relationship with men. The woman who depends on her husband to succeed for her has never tested herself. The woman who has taken chances and achieved for herself can only gain a measure of self-esteem. Her position in life is the proof.

Some of us may have had fathers who were distant during our early childhoods, when we were intent on wooing Daddy, but who mellowed and came around for us during adolescence. Others may have had adoring fathers before the age of five or six and discovered them to be cold, critical, and seriously conflicted at the onset of puberty.

"I can still see my father's face before me the moment my mother told my father I'd gotten my period," one woman said. "He paled and looked shocked, betrayed, and I don't know what else. I was only ten years old, really a baby, though I looked four years older. I was definitely Daddy's girl. My sisters were my mother's girls. Our relationship ended that day. We barely spoke to each other for the next eight years, except to quarrel about the state of my room. My mother told me that I was a woman when I got my period, but I didn't want to be one if it meant my father's withdrawal. For years I was petrified to have a relationship, fearing rejection because I *was* a woman."

FIGURING FATHER OUT

How would you evaluate your childhood with your father? Which kind of daughter were you—adored or deprived? Are you still looking for a father? Did you allow your father to have faults—to be real—or is he still your hero? Are you a woman who needs constant attention? Now take a look at how your father treated your mother. What was the nature of their relationship? Did he put your needs before hers? Was he overly warm and loving to you? Or was he denying and cold?

And what of your husband? Do you notice any similarity between your parent's marriage and your own? Are you always asking for more than your husband is willing to give? Does what he give you always seem less than enough? Do you find yourself always angry with him? What are the reasons for that anger? Are you looking for a free ride in your marriage? Do you assume the little-girl role and expect him to do everything for you while you, in return, do nothing? Are you in competition with your husband, hoping to show him up? Are you anxious for your husband to outshine your father in order to prove that you could attract a better man than he is?

Certain people inspire us to be one way when we are with them, another way without them. One person may descirbe us as shy, another as ebullient. Who are the men you've selected and what did they bring out in you? A desire to nurture? Good humor, argumentativeness, detachment, fear, distrust, desire, friendship, or loathing? Who were the men who brought out the better side of you? Is your husband one of the men who enriched your life by encouraging your more productive or compassionate side? If a partner brings out characteristics that are to your detriment, don't try to rehabilitate him. But don't run from the truth. If, in fact, you are like oil and water together, would you be better off with him as a friend, and not as a husband? If he recreates your situation with your father, and your relationship with your father has prevented emotional growth, do you really need it?

Are you still behaving toward your father as you did when

you were a little girl or a teen-ager? Do you know how to anger him, threaten him with a withdrawal of your love, play on his weaknesses to get your way? A single woman I know jousts with her father each time she sees him. "Daddy, I met a man, but you're not going to like him," she says, strategically preparing for the battle that is to come. "He's an out-of-work actor who lives in a van—but he's terrific!" Father, automatically responding to the prod, jumps in for the skirmish. "Are you out of your mind?" he shouts. "How serious is this? Don't think I'm about to feed the both of you."

Your father is the man he is, and he may know no other way. *You* still have a chance to change by learning how to address the issues to him and having some compassion for him as a *person*. Once you alter his approach, you can begin to break the bond with him. If he's a remote father, understand that he didn't have the ability to demonstrate fatherhood—then and perhaps now. We cannot go back and hope that this time we can bounce on his knee. Often, daughters of distant fathers summon the courage to tell their fathers that no matter what they've done, they're still loved. This touching confession may stir a father to a like response or cause him to react cruelly out of guilt or fear. A friend of mine told of such a reaction. "Daddy," a woman told her father, whom she hadn't seen in ten years, "I want you to know I care and that I think we should be friends." He replied, "You're still not included in my will."

The indulgent father may not appreciate his daughter's marrying a man who can provide what she needs. He's the father who will go to a department store for a tie and wind up having an entire living-room suite sent to his daughter. Why? She mentioned that she and her husband were saving for new furniture. It's difficult to turn down limitless generosity when it's become second nature to accept it, but the "daddy's girl" will doom her marriage unless she learns to say no to him. If this father flies into a rage, that's his problem. What he wants to do is keep you in your place, not for your sake, but for his. As painful as it is to reject this father's smothering love, the "daddy's girl" must understand that her husband, and what he can provide, is what is important, first and foremost.

Why is it so important for you to analyze your relationship with your father? Roles in marriage become fixed in the early stages and become more difficult to change as time goes on. In my practice, a woman may tell me about an argument with her husband that happened fifteen years ago, the affair he had ten years ago, how he was insensitive to her three years ago. To these women, fifteen, ten, or three years ago is the same as yesterday. Why? They never fully resolved the issues when they arose, therefore their backs are bent, so to speak, from hauling around a lifetime of injustices committed against them. Few of us resolve problems with our parents, and we don't resolve problems with our husbands.

Do you want your father to change his behavior toward you? He will, but not from any change that arises independently within him. Behave toward your father in the same way you wish to be treated, stop reacting according to the old patterns, and he'll catch on. Let's see what my taunting friend would say to her father about dating an out-of-work actor. This is clearly a relationship where a father is interested in his daughter's social life. So, instead of her provoking him with information that will obviously anger him, all she need do is wait for him to ask about the men in her life. "Are you dating anyone special?" he may ask. "No," she must say as an adult woman, "not anyone I'd bring home to meet you . . . yet." And change the subject.

When you do become an adult, you can tolerate the ambivalences you feel about a parent. You will recognize the flaws and accept them and go on to change yourself. When you perceive your parents as lifelong authority figures, unpleasant feelings erupt. A woman who harbors what Dr. Appleton calls a "binding hate" toward a parent will spend her days emotionally attached to that parent. Because of that bond, she isn't free to find significant men who will fulfill her. She'll want unending approval, attention, love; she'll demand money, flattery, and no criticism. Until she cuts that bond to her father, she may never drain her reservoir of hurt feelings.

Few of our fathers had expectations of us greater than that we should be good, responsible, tending women. Our expectations of them may have been out of proportion to what they are. Father did what he could. Now it's your chance.

Chapter Five

Bite the Hand That Feeds You

"All those writers who talk about their childhood!" she said bitterly. "Gentle God, if I ever wrote about mine, you wouldn't sit in the same room with me."
—John Keats, You Might As Well Live/The Life and Times of Dorothy Parker

Your health is bound to be affected if, day after day, you say the opposite of what you feel, if you grovel before what you dislike and rejoice at what brings you nothing but misfortune. . . . Our souls cannot be forever violated with impunity.
—Boris Pasternak, Doctor Zhivago

Not only do we become accustomed to the manner in which our parents have always treated us, but we recreate that connectedness to them with the men we marry. Though it's not a universal phenomenon, most women who are unhappy in their relationships with their parents are unhappy with their husbands in a remarkably similar way. Still caught in that parental net; still acting on old responses that make us angry, fretful, fearful, doubtful, that make us feel like nothings; still seeking parental approval; we transfer all those unresolved feelings onto a man. Trapped in those problematic family rhythms, we have little choice but to select a mate who will nearly duplicate the authority role by replaying our parents' attitudes toward us. The distinction between our role as child in the family and our role as wife in marriage is a slim one.

Aware of the deeply rooted negative image we had of ourselves within the family, many of us swore to find men who would be loving where our parents were not. Try though we might, we did not hold fast to that vow. Consciously or unconsciously, we were drawn to men who took over where our parents left off. Such marriages that mirrored the past could be grim reminders of what once was—dubious attractions and irritations included.

Perhaps you have yearned to break your negative connections with your family, but have not succeeded. Some women I know have simply cut off all communication with their parents, thinking this will resolve the conflicts. It doesn't. These women can burn stacks of family photos, slam down the phone when they hear their mothers' or fathers' voices on the other end, and even declare themselves orphans to the world, but really, Mom and Dad are still a depressing preoccupation with them. Physical disassociation, they learn by experience, does not guarantee emotional freedom from parents. Some lose patience around parents and act out different versions of the same old quarrels. Others concede the battles and automatically apologize to parents for living: "Sorry, Mom. Sorry, Dad. I'm not the kid you hoped for."

Breaking negative bonds with parents is not an easy task. But getting over the negativism, the left-over attitudes and habits we played out with our parents, is not impossible. *It can be done.* Most of all, though, it requires a willingness to take an objective look at one's parents' marriage and one's own relationship with them. If you make peace with history, you can free yourself from its destructive influence. Otherwise, you could be working through the same neurotic patterns with your husband and children, hoping to get from them the reactions you wanted from your parents. But those positive reactions won't be forthcoming if you're still bound to your parents. For example, if you were the much-maligned victim of the family, the man in your life will most likely not be a generous, giving sort, but someone who will accommodate himself to your need to feel put upon. And you will cooperate in the game if that's the only way you know.

Parents who are consumed by feelings of extreme inadequacy or powerlessness have only their own self-doubts to pass on. A meager legacy, most would admit—qualities, we'd say, not worthy of our identifying with. But their admirable qualities somehow got lost in the guilt, pathos, and adversity of family life. Frankly, we now spend too much time counting the disagreeable traits in our parents and either overlook or dismiss the praiseworthy attributes. And they *are* there, slight though they may be in some cases, but worth finding.

You don't have to spend your life resenting your parents or wishing they would change. You must change your reactions toward them. How? Let's begin by making an attempt to understand, first, the truth about your parents' marriage, viewed by you not as a child but as an adult observer, and, second, the effect of their marriage on you and how it determined your choice of a man.

Describe your mother and father—not physically, but according to the kinds of people they were. Did they both adhere to a single behavioral pattern, or did they act in radically different ways?

"My father was a tyrannical man," one Boston woman told me, "with hard and fast rules about how to live. My mother was his opposite—a little scatterbrained, artistic, someone who found her way out of difficulties with a quick wit. They fought all the time, but I knew it was less to destroy each other than to establish her little-girlishness and his total command. I grew up believing that anger and hostility in a man concealed a vast love. It may have been true of my parents, but it's rarely been proved true for me." Another reported: "My father was a meek, shy man who had a terrific drive to be liked. He was nice to a fault. My mother called the shots, handled the money, even picked out his clothes and his brand of deodorant. I wanted a man who was as kind as he was, but with a bit more gumption."

Did your parents impart to you a general "philosophy of life"? For instance: "Get what you can and give as little as you have to in return, because no one does anything for anyone but himself." "Life is nothing but hardship and struggle." "Don't be too curious—you'll ask for trouble and get it." "Be like us." "Look for the best in people and don't get discouraged if you fail."

What do you think of their marriage? Is it the kind of marriage you would like to have? Is it, in fact, the kind of marriage you *do* have?

"My parents both had enormous feelings of insecurity," one woman told me. "They were terrified of poverty and hoarded every penny. We were always told that we were

114

poor, though I found out later they had a fortune in the bank. Money was their god. If I wanted something, I had to work for it—and I've been working since I was fourteen years old. I married a man who was the opposite. He's irresponsible with money—a man who'd buy a new car instead of paying the mortgage on the house, or a new suit for himself rather than shoes for the kids. Though my parents were misers and my husband a spendthrift, I wound up in the same position of not having, and worrying about every penny."

To which parent do you think you're more similar? "I'm kind of like my mother." "I feel the way my father did—that no matter how you try to get ahead, someone will pull the rug out from under you." "I'm selfish like my mother." "I have my father's ability to make friends."

Which of the two of them do you like better, and why? "My father had a wonderful sense of adventure and playfulness. I felt happy in his company. My mother was usually there to put an end to any fun." "My mother was enormously kind. Everyone liked her. I was proud of her popularity." "My father was a gentle man who wasn't good at showing affection, but you never doubted that he cared. My mother had a vicious streak in her. You never knew when she'd turn on you."

Did one parent say, "You're just like your father/mother," meaning it in a derogatory way? "You have a mind of your own, just like *him*." "I don't know where you got the idea to be a dancer. Not from *me*." "No one on *my* side of the family is a dreamer" (or "has a weight problem," or "has a moody disposition").

What is your earliest memory involving both of them?

"My parents had a horrible fight right before they split up," a Detroit woman said. "I was about four years old then. My mother was sitting on the bed, crying, and I remember putting my fingers in her ears so she wouldn't have to hear what my father was shouting at her. Then I can picture my father going to a mirror to put a Band-Aid across the bridge of his nose. I must have asked him why, because I recall his answering that my mother threw a chair at him."

What your parents complain about? "Your father doesn't give me enough money." "Your mother is a slob." "I can't take your father anywhere. He embarrasses me." "Your mother is cold and won't let me touch her."

Did they insist that you be like your siblings?

"I was raised to be the kind of woman my brother Roger would marry," a New York woman said. "He was the gem of the family—smart, good-looking, the kind of boy who was always smiling. My parents compared me to him with every step I took. They even said I wore too much makeup and looked like a tramp. *Roger* wouldn't be seen with me."

Is there a difference between the collective message they gave you and the way they lived?

"My mother was obsessed with sex and warned me about having sex before marriage," a friend confided to me. "She made sex out to be the foulest act any human could commit. Then I found out from my father that she'd gone to bed with him before they married—and I could have strangled her! She doomed me to a very bad sexual relationship with my husband because I couldn't overcome her voice telling me no, no, no! Becoming a sexual being has almost been a lifetime chore for me."

Could you discuss any confusion you had about something important in your life without the fear of being chastised or made to feel foolish or even more confused?

"I wanted to get married," a Connecticut wife said, "because I wanted to have a home and share my life. But I was also worried about a man taking me over and making all my decisions. When I told my mother how I felt, she replied, 'Really, dear. He's not going to take over your life. He's just going to help you the way *we* helped you.' "

Did your parents always feel they knew what was best for you? Did you lose a sense of security in making your own decisions or forfeit a chance to test yourself?

"Why do you want to be a singer?" one mother asked her daughter, who'd mentioned that she wanted to leave home to study voice. "What's wrong with singing in the choir on Sundays and teaching school during the week? If you stay home, you won't be hurt by disappointment when you don't get a job. Think about it. Isn't my way smarter?" Her daughter stayed with the choir.

What did your parents hope to have in life before they were married? Are they happy with the way things turned out? If not, why not?

"My mother wanted to marry a dynamic man who'd give her a life of ease," an Illinois woman said. "My father wanted to succeed for her, but failed at three or four businesses. She was always at him to make something of himself, directing him. He was bitter and exhausted by the time he was fifty-five years old, and my mother thought she'd thrown her life away on a failure. I often heard her say she wished she'd married her first boyfriend, who became a pharmacist. I know my father loved her early on and probably needed a woman like her to push him, for whatever reasons. She pushed him once too often and he left her. Now he works as a salesman for an appliance chain and likes it. He's thrilled not to have that pressure on him any longer."

Did you feel that you were loved and lovable? Were you made to feel that you were a basically decent, good human being with failings, or a nobody who'd always be a problem?

"My mother wouldn't let me do anything for myself," a New York woman said, "then she'd accuse me of being inept, clumsy, stupid, or lazy. My father discouraged any ambition on my part and told me I'd be lucky if any man married me. I felt I could never please them, and if I did, I almost waited to be shot down."

Were you able to excuse yourself from situations that you thought were not in your best interests? Were you rewarded for deeds that didn't make you feel good inside? Did you feel that you were being asked to deny your own feelings and sense of appropriateness?

"My mother didn't want me to have any friends and always found something wrong with each of them. She forbade me to visit them and to invite them to our house. In return, she'd take me shopping with her and buy me something I didn't need."

Did your parents support you in your efforts and responses?

"I'd wanted to be an artist since I was very young," a New York woman told me. "To my parents, this was synonymous with being a degenerate. To discourage me, I was not bought any art supplies. I wanted to go to a specialized high school where I could major in art. My parents refused to let me go. So I forged my mother's signature to the note that allowed me to take the test, and prepared a portfolio at a friend's house. When I was told that I'd gotten into the high school, my father said I still couldn't go. I again forged a note, this time giving myself permission to go to the school of my choice. When September rolled around, my father asked when I'd be starting at the local high school. I said I wasn't going there, but to the art school I'd gotten into, and if they didn't want me to go there, they could very well call the principal and explain it to him. I went to the school I chose. Belatedly, they admired me for having talent—although only after others affirmed that I did."

How did your parents treat each other? Did they allow each other to be themselves? Did they appreciate their differences and similarities? Did they approve of each other genuinely as people?

"Both of my parents had a position about everything," a Detroit woman said. "Each of them had to be right all the time. There was no such thing as compromise, just defeat. One would give in to the other when things got too rough. They fought over the smallest detail. Once my mother placed a bottle of beer in the center of the table, instead of next to my father's plate. This got my father furious. He accused her of being incompetent at laying out a dinner by making him reach an extra six inches for the beer. Their relationship was all quibbling, bickering, or full-blown arguments."

How do you think they would describe you? Mother's reaction: "My mother doesn't understand my single life-style, but I think she's secretly proud of me." Father's reaction:

"My father never thought I'd earn more than he does. He worries that I won't get married."

What do you want from your parents now? "I would like them to stop criticizing me and accept me as I am." "I wish they'd calm down and like each other and not use us kids to mediate their battles."

Now that you've answered these questions—or at least begun to think about them—you'll be aware of how much of your parents' philosophy you truly subscribe to. By looking at their marriage, you may be able to learn precisely where you pick up their patterns and how you enact a similar version of them in your life. You may not want to admit it, but you may well be repeating the patterns your parents have set up for themselves. If you're dissatisfied with a life that too faithfully resembles this candid portrait of your parents, there's still an opportunity for you to change what you don't like. How? Hold an image of your parents in front of you and match yourself with them, point for point. By not doing this analysis of your parent's marriage, you're asking for a similar destiny.

Here are some ways in which the patterns may emerge:

If you wanted something, perhaps your parents accused you of being greedy, demanding, or selfish. Now that you're married, you hesitate to do anything for yourself because your husband and children will say the same of you. You still deny yourself little pleasures and greater achievements.

Your parents may have poked fun at your feelings, either by insisting that you were imagining slights or that you should grow up and stop being overly sensitive about nothing. Now that you're married, you may still be ridiculed for showing that you've been hurt. You may even have come to believe that you're oversensitive, and not that a husband or child who ridicules your feelings is being insensitive. Conversely, you may have decided never to show your feelings at all, except when you're pleased. Over the years, even those pleasurable feelings may be completely stifled.

Did your parents deal with issues through prolonged fighting, silences, or a withholding of money, sex, or love? Now that you're married, you may confront issues by doing the same with your husband. Or your husband may be very like your parents and involve you in the kind of arguments that were all too familiar to you while growing up.

GROWING UP: WHO ARE YOU GOING TO BE

Even as adults, a part of us yearns to have our parents not only take care of us but approve of all we do. The child in us is still acting out, though we may be technically and legally "adults." Having been a certain kind of child with our parents, we either want that status to continue or discontinue. Many women want to be passively involved in their own lives so others may take charge of them—a task first assumed by parents, then by a husband, then possibly by all three, working as a committee.

"I did not want to grow up," a Milwaukee woman confessed, "and give up the privileges of childhood. My parents doted on me and told me that everything I did was wonderful! I went through a terrible adolescence, mostly wishing that time would stop for me. I hated having my period. I resented growing taller and developing breasts. I threw ugly tantrums and made demands like a four-year-old. When I

121

reached seventeen, I began to calm down, but I still looked to my parents for everything. They wanted me to go away to college, to get out of the house and be on my own for a while. They practically had to drag me bodily to an out-of-town school.

"I married at twenty, to a man five years older than myself, and looked to him to care for me. I've been married for fifteen years now, and in all that time I've done nothing but feel relief that I'm not on my own and, at the same time, that I may have to be. I'm like my mother. I need a man to lean on and tell me that I'm okay. I want my husband always to feel toward me the way my father feels toward my mother—devoted."

Other women, less dependent and less the recipient of vast amounts of parental approval, are equally baffled at the prospect of taking care of themselves. Such women may be troubled because they too don't know who they are except as they are defined by their parents. They do know how they fit within the family, but unlike more clinging women, they are ruled by negative messages. For both of them, there was a period when they tried on personalities, experimented, and looked to a parent to help form and define their identities.

There is a prevailing—and, I think, erroneous—theory of psychology that tells us we are to identify with one parent or the other: a girl to her mother, a boy to his father. In truth, our identity is formed by relating to qualities in both of them. If we're healthy, we identify with *positive* aspects of both the mother and the father. We may have gestures like our fathers', or our taste in food may be like our mothers'; we may have our fathers' physical constitutions and our mothers' sensitivities; we may have our fathers' dispositions and our mothers' intellectual capacities.

Sociologist Philip Slater, in his book *Footholds*, addresses the complex issue of identification through his theory of "personal" or "positional" identification. The process of "personal" identification results, says Slater, "when a child adopts the personality traits, values, and attitudes of a parent, including the parent's view of the child. . . . It is motivated by the child's love and admiration for the parent. The child says, in effect, I want to be like you and love myself as much as I love you."

So, while personal identification is based on a child's need to take in the qualities that are admired in a parent, "positional" love is based on adopting a few characteristics that symbolize the parent's position of power. Slater goes on: "Positional identification involves merely a fantasy of putting oneself in the other's position and acting out the appropriate role. It is motivated not by love, but by fear and envy. The child is saying, in effect, I wish I were in your shoes. If I were, I wouldn't be in the unpleasant position I am in now. If I act like you, I will achieve your more favorable status."

When there is parental affection, the child will tend to model herself after the loved parents and therefore assume personal identification. In the absence of parental affection, the positional view will take over, with the child imitating a few characteristics that she believes will endow her with some *power*. Many of these characteristics are the very ones that get us into trouble.

We may choose to see power as being founded on argumentativeness, denial of emotional or material rewards, lack of consideration for others' feelings or desires, empty promises and threats, deviousness, coldhearted manipulation, narcissism, or grudging approval. So the child who says "I wish I were in your shoes" picks and chooses with utmost concern for her survival within the family any number of these tactics with which to fight the parent. When the parent forces emotionally loaded power plays on the child, the child responds in kind. Before long, they relate to each other only as adversaries.

Sadly, as we get older, characteristics of positional identification become second nature. Marriage has a tendency to bring them out in full force. Should a husband attempt any of these emotionally loaded power plays, we automatically counter them as we did with our parents—through argument, denial, malevolence, or demeaning of the other person. Yet, though we may replay with our husbands the conflicts of our parents, many of us have promised not to treat our children as we were treated by our parents. Not surprisingly, the old patterns emerge anyway.

Marcia, a Los Angeles mother, told me: "I promised I wouldn't hit my kids because when I was a child I was beaten. When my daughter was born, I had very little to give her. At that time I still believed in the premise that if you're not shown love, you don't give it easily. When my daughter would get to me, I'd grab her by the shoulders, practically throw her into the room, clench my teeth, and say, 'I'm now about to save your life. If I lay one hand on you, you'll never survive!' There was this fear in me that I would become a torturer like my mother was. Well, what was it all about? It took me until I was forty-two years old to figure out that my mother's life was a tragedy of her own making. If I ever asked for anything, she felt such deprivation and jealousy that all she could do was either deny it to me, give it grudgingly, or pummel me. She was full of anger about her life and fearful that I might have something she couldn't."

The negative messages received from parents, neatly tied up in a not-very-pretty package, are often indirect evaluations of the parents themselves, projected onto the children. The parent may say, "Can't you do anything right?" The unspoken message is, *I'm afraid of being wrong.* The parent may say, "Men only use you for one thing." The unspoken message: *I sold myself out to a man I didn't love. The same thing won't happen to you.* The parent may say, "You're no good." The unspoken message: *I'm no good, so you can't be any better.*

There are many children who have survived terrible parental abuse and neglect and have grown up to lead productive, happy lives. These are the "invulnerables"—children who managed through inner strength and unwavering intention to fight for their own identities. What did they do? At some critical point in their development, they distanced themselves from their parents and vowed, "I won't be like them, and *I'm going to make it.*" As children, they received destructive messages and even worse treatment from their parents. Good enough reason, it would seem, for them to wander through life with scarcely enough self-esteem to hold a job. But these mistreated children are not the ones who became outcasts or backsliders—though they may have been judged black sheep, renegades, or delinquents. Instead of becoming the oppositional, rebellious, negative type, some transformed themselves into the oppositional, rebellious *positive.* In a less extreme version, many women who were tormented children have courageously surpassed their parents' expectations of them.

"I was told that I'd never amount to anything unless some man married me, and I'd be lucky at that," a New York businesswoman confided. "But I knew I had something in me to succeed; where it came from, I can't tell you. I'm an executive at a large corporation, and now my mother asks my younger sisters, 'Why can't you be like Franny?' The irony is that my mother didn't want me to have an education, but to work right after high school and bring money into the house. I worked part time, but went to school anyway.

"My mother thought of me as rebellious, overreaching, a troublemaker. My father either ignored me or criticized me. Now that I've gotten somewhere, my parents nag my sisters to apply themselves to do as well. My parents have rearranged the facts in their minds so they can take the credit for my achievement. Naturally my sisters resent me for the opportunities I had as the eldest child. What opportunities? I made them all myself, fighting all the way. I've often wondered where I'd be if I *hadn't* come from a home where my parents denied me kindness and support. If I look at my life objectively, I can see that I got my fighting spirit from both of them, but managed to channel it differently."

Transforming adversity into a positive force, Franny improved her life. Rather than succumb to the negative messages and seek affirmation within a marriage that was supposed to make someone out of her, she challenged the messages—and won.

Remember, there are only a few issues that provoke us to

combat, and those issues involve power—who is going to control whom. David Klimek, Ph.D., in *Beneath Mate Selection and Marriage,* posits that troubled individuals "who feel that no one cares and that they don't matter to anyone are almost always in a power struggle. There is a natural and predictable human phenomenon that forces those who feel the most insignificant to seek positions of power. To control others is *to matter."*

What does this theory mean for us?

When a woman has grown up in a home where she has mastered positional identification—that is, identifying with the behavior of the feared or envied parent—the old negative messages resonate within her. Often, as an adult, she doesn't behave generously toward others and denies them satisfaction. Part of the response is automatic; another part is a conscious effort to gain satisfaction for herself by not giving what has not been given to her. If, as a child, she said to her parents, "My teacher said to tell you I'm an asset to the class," the positional parental response may have been, "No one likes a goody-goody." So today, if her husband says, "You promised to make blueberry pancakes this Sunday," her positional adult response may well be, "Why should I fuss for the lot of you? What does anyone do for me?"

What is beneath this anger? Responses like this one are motivated by anger. Does it arise from a belief that happiness comes from denying or demeaning others? Does it spring from a conviction that controlling others' actions and moods is the only way to feel as if one matters?

When you care about yourself and for yourself, you can cut loose such negative attitudes. If you feel the heat rising between you and a parent, husband, or child and are about to swat that person literally or figuratively, swallow the impulse. Question the other person's motives. What is the reaction this parent, spouse, or child is trying to elicit from you? Are you supposed to feel in the wrong? Unlovable? Irrational? Uninformed, therefore stupid? Selfish? Incapable of making a just decision? The thing to keep in mind is that you must not react in the way that's expected of you.

We often see parents as powerful, when in fact they are weak and unsure of themselves. When parents have to step back so a son or daughter can step forward, they will reach into their bag of tricks to prove they still have some purpose, usefulness, and a bit of power. Becoming overwhelmed by a parent as a matter of habit, and reacting from the positional stance, is self-defeating. The more child there is in us, the more likely we are to look to our parents for direction while trying to usurp their control. The truth of the matter, of course, is that they really can't take over our lives.

There will come a time when you must acknowledge that your parents will never be the people you hoped they would be. When you accept that, you will be on your way to greater wisdom and emotional health. In reality, you don't have to go back and master the past through the present. When you attempt to exercise that bit of complicated psychology, you are still dealing with your parents as if you were a child, not as you are now—an adult. Rather, a woman should try to examine the reasonable expectations she has of her parents. Should they be taking care of her the way her husband hasn't? Should they be making her decisions? Should they approve of everything she does or thinks? They should not! Then what's the answer?

The Ten Commandments are very cleverly drawn. Nowhere do they say, "Thou shalt *love* thy mother and father," but simply, "Thou shalt *honor* thy mother and father." Your parents were good enough to let you survive, caring for you when you were young and helpless. Now you can add some dignity to their lives with kindness. You needn't love them, but you can offer them compassion, even compassionate anger, with respect. The feelings they engendered in you—good or bad—are *your* feelings, to change or not to change. Recognize, though, that the past is over. Your parents raised you as they knew how; that you'd have preferred better or different parents is beside the point.

Your entire genetic heritage comes from your parents. If you understand and accept your parents for who they are, and yourself for who you are, your only obligation is to say to them, in effect, "Thanks, I'll take it from here."

When you see your parents as if they were distinguished strangers, you can treat them with a certain etiquette and sense of moral obligation. This noblesse oblige may make the relationship a politely strained one, but if you've resolved to stay in contact with them—and in the only way you know how—then this is what must be. Moral obligation, if nothing else, ends the torture that comes from repeating the same arguments over and over again.

I've known of women who, even in their forties, are unable to have compassion for their parents, unable to perceive who their parents are and what they haven't had out of life. These women continue to harp on what was denied them. Some, still in competition with their mothers at this advanced age, find satisfaction in pointing out how they've triumphed while their mothers have not. "Look at what my husband buys for me," a woman like this may boast to her mother. "What does yours give you?" Others, bound to their fathers by strong feelings of contempt, will remark to them, "Keep your advice. What do you know about taking care of a wife?" Such cruel jibes are unnecessary at this stage of life. Your history with your parents cannot be amended, rectified, or refashioned to suit a more ideal vision.

BECOMING A GOOD PARENT TO YOURSELF

Good parenting is based on a simple concept, as mentioned earlier. Teach children to walk, and then to walk away. A good parent puts herself out of a job by giving a child the ability to negotiate the waters of life. Good parenting is done with love, guidance, and discipline; none of these three requisites should be abused. Given some parents' persistence in being the perpetual control center of their children's lives, these guidelines can easily be ignored. Some parents may be ardently devoted to unconditional love. This means the child is never wrong but always right, because the parent has too large an emotional investment in her. Whether or not they seriously mean to do so, some parents use the concept of guidance to break the child's spirit or destroy her will. Hemmed in by rigorous rules, the child can't step out of fixed boundaries without fear of punishment. Discipline, to some punitive parents, implies beatings, humiliation, and the taking away of privileges for extended periods.

A child's needs are simple: to feel wanted and protected; to feel she can explore and experience the world, and do so with prudent guidance. Most important, a child needs to know that she is okay as she is—faults and all. The parent who doesn't allow the child any flaws doesn't allow him- or herself any flaws either. The parent will inevitably have faults—who doesn't?—but will simply deny their existence.

What does a child have the right to expect from a parent? As an infant, the child has the right to be totally cared for during this most vulnerable period. The toddler has the right to experiment with a variety of situations while being protected from danger. In grade school the child has the right to expect guidance in the areas of socialization, good study habits, and respect and appreciation for authority. In high school the child has the right to expect accurate information about sex and positive messages about love and responsibility, as well as guidance in preparing for a job or career goal. At this last stage, a parent must understand that the teen-ager will try out a number of identities: the rebel, the "good girl," the scholar, the performer, the shy violet. Though it's a confusing time, a supportive parent will aid the child in seeking out her true identity so that she may confidently go out into the world.

The picture of ideal parenthood may be fuzzy around the edges for most of us. We may have received guidance in growing up, though not in quite so positive a way. Even though we're adults now, married and with our own children, very likely we still need a mother and father. This bond to a parent may not be based on fondness but on resentment; unfortunately, it is still a bond. And if that bond, for better or for worse, is one that is important to our functioning, or affects the way we relate to others, there are going to be some problems. We want parents to treat us like adults; often they don't. Instead we have to start *behaving* like adults if we are to loosen the bond.

Our parents too have suffered a lack of positive training from their own parents. But if they are like most of us, they've done the best they know how. Therefore, for you to undo some of the poor parenting you received from them and not repeat their errors with your own children, you must understand the nature of parenting and renounce the patterns that stifle growth. It's not too late to become the parent you always wanted *for* yourself, *by* yourself, to give *to* yourself.

Very often, when there's a conflict with a parent, a woman will find a man whose personality is both malleable and *unlike* the parent she does not want to be like. This woman will try to shape a man into the feared, loved, or resented parent, and endow him with all the characteristics she needs to master something from the past. Here is an illustration of this principle:

During courtship, Brad, the man Judy cared for, took charge of the evening's events. Judy liked that because her own father was passive and allowed her mother to run their family life. After a while Judy got annoyed with Brad's doing all the planning; she wanted some input. So Judy made reservations for dinner, and accepted an invitation to a late-night party. Brad concurred with her decisions. At this point, Judy and Brad had struck a nice balance: Both were contributing. It became a bit exhilarating for Judy, and she thought, *Why do what Brad wants to do? Why not what I want to do—all the time!*

Slowly but surely, Judy started to erode Brad's participation in the relationship—often without being aware of it. She began to mime her mother, despite her vow that she'd never do so. And here was Brad—a nice, agreeable chap who was unaware that he was in the middle of a convoluted personal drama. Before long, Judy made all the arrangements, while Brad remained affable and happy to please her. One day, Judy turned around and charged him with being passive by saying, "When was the last time you made an effort to handle the arrangements? Why is it always up to me?" Is Brad at fault? Not in this case. A man less agreeable than Brad might have spoken up when he realized that his life was being planned by someone else, but this was not in Brad's makeup. The question of who made the arrangements was less significant to him than the opportunity to be with Judy.

When you reenact through a man the problems you had with your parents, he becomes a pawn in your game of trying to get back *to,* and *at,* your parents. What benefits are there to finding a healthy man and making him unhealthy by changing the game on him? None. In a healthy marriage, partners can change roles. There is a recognition between them that at various times one is more assertive than the other and takes the reins; for instance, one does the child-rearing and the other goes out to work. This kind of couple is not locked into role stereotypes or negative parental messages that need to be played out again and again. Such couples don't become involved in power struggles as much as in goal struggles; that is, one will not tell the other what to do, but they may argue over how both of them will get to where they want to be.

Your biological parents may not have given you a good model with which to identify, nor provided you with a basis for developing self-esteem. Part of re-parenting yourself out of a negative mold and into a positive one is to find a *psychological* parent—a person you hold in esteem, whose example you would like to follow. The psychological parent will function much like a mentor and will play the part of the good parent. The point is to establish some emotional connection to that person whose humanity, courage, or positive outlook will both inspire and influence you. The psychological mother or father can be someone you know, a celebrity you admire for qualities other than the obvious glamour he or she possesses, or someone you've read about who either actually exists or is a character in a novel. This will be your new parent for now.

Diana found her psychological parents when she was fifteen. Her own parents, who divorced when she was four years old, had little contact with each other. Diana saw her father every four or five years, and each meeting was further proof to her that she was neither loved nor cared about by him. Her mother, unable to come to grips with the divorce, treated Diana shabbily.

"I became friends with a girl at school and she invited me home to dinner," Diana recounted. "That dinner changed my life. Helen's mother was a working woman, kind to her children, and she wasn't beautiful—a fact that was important to me at the time, since I felt so unattractive. Helen's father appeared to adore his wife, and the only time he had hit his daughter, Diana told me, was when she had made a nasty crack about her mother. To me, Helen's mother was nearly perfect, no matter that Helen thought her too strict. Here was a woman, a mother, who took an interest in me, told me I was bright, and encouraged me to do something with my life. I was in awe of her. Here was a man, a father, who cherished his wife and showed it! I was in love with him. They both became the parents I didn't have, and the thought of them got me through all kinds of hell at home. Knowing people like these made me want to strive for something like what they had."

Of course, if you select a psychological parent you can talk to, relate to, and see in action, it will be so much more to your benefit. The psychological parent need not know that he or she has been chosen for this role—or even that you exist. What matters is how you interact with that person if he or she is real, or how you think you would interact if that person were a part of your life. The psychological parent, if real, offers a sense of trust and allows you to be yourself. The woman who chooses a model who's inaccessible can say to herself, "Would Mary think I was making the right decision? How would Mary handle this?"

Although it would be ideal to have a daily, ongoing relationship with a psychological parent, it's not necessary. If you take in all the good feelings (actual or imagined) so you can recall them at will, the intensity of the relationship can be sustained even if you only see that person once or twice a year—or never. The affirmation he or she gives you can carry you through until the next time you need support. And when your model parent cannot be met or spoken to, you can, in your mind, create that same kind of approval to move you toward emotional growth.

Negative messages have an extraordinary impact on us and tend to cancel out positive ones. Your real father may have perpetuated the myth that you were nothing; your psychological father has never believed there is anything you can't do. Which one will you believe? Who knows you best? How do you sort out the truth of these conflicting messages? Which father do you choose to reward by being who you are—nothing or something? We've played out old, destructive messages in our minds for decades, and they've taken hold. This doesn't mean they can't be cancelled and new, positive messages fed in. Our parents may have had an unfortunate marriage and given us messages that stopped us from going forward and fulfilling ourselves. Right now it's not important. Those messages don't have to continue playing, sabotaging you in the process, as long as you find an example of a good parent, listen, and take in the good messages and begin to *live* them.

Some of us are lucky—we have a biological and psychological parent wrapped up in one. Most of us, however, have a more diffuse picture. During the course of a lifetime, we may have many psychological parents, but we will always have two biological ones. The biological parents deserve from us respect for giving us the gift of life. The psychological parent may receive many more rewards for having been supportive of us in our successes and generous with praise and love. In some ways, we're richer for having these many psychological parents whom we did not know totally. Instead, we can select those qualities that are worth modeling ourselves after. Those of us who spend most of our lives hating our parents can only count an execrable waste of time, energy, and misdirected emotion. If I could save someone from even six months of this kind of hate, I would be happy.

It is not only the psychological parent who can help us; we can turn the corner to emotional growth through positive "self-talk," which allows one's self-esteem to develop. A person's concept of self evolves over a lifetime. It's not something that's left to chance or station of birth, nor is it finalized at one stage of life, imprinted as a permanent code and fixed forever, never to be changed in any way. "The greatest discovery of my generation," William James said at the turn of the century, "is that human beings may alter their lives by altering their attitudes of mind." This seems an easy enough concept to comprehend, but it is mind-bogglingly difficult for many of us to believe. However, consider this: If you assume the attitude that others have power over you, and that your parents or society's injustices have forced you to be the way you are, and therefore they and everyone else must suffer for it, then you have essentially lost control over yourself. Someone else has you in the palm of his hand.

Low self-esteem frequently results from frustration, inaction, our own disbelief concerning what we can and can't accomplish, and dread that we will not measure up to another's standards, no matter how lofty or lowly those standards may be. It may also result from a fixation on performance, which disallows mistakes and creates a daunting fear of failure.

The person of low self-esteem holds a picture of herself as an inferior being, often hoping all the while that others will not find out. Yet this sense of inferiority is revealed by comments like, "Nothing I do is right, so why try something else?" Or "My parents didn't love me, so why should I show love to anyone else?" Or "So what if I hurt people. Haven't *I* been hurt?"

I met a woman once who has a desk full of children's stories she's afraid to send out to a publisher. What's stopping her? To this woman, rejection would spell catastrophe. She is unable to see that perhaps by sending out a story or two, she might have the chance to get what she wants—a story in print. Rather than think of herself as an unpublished writer of children's stories, she believes herself to be a *failed* one.

But how could she be a failed writer if she's made no effort to get her work in print? Even if her work is rejected, there may be, along with a rejection note, some suggestions that might improve her work and make it saleable. Is she really more satisfied and safe within her image of herself as a failure than she would be if she proved that she was not?

To change your self-concept, you need to change your behavior and attitudes. Behave like someone who's worthy of respect, love, and admiration, and you will be treated accordingly. Recognize that although you have failed at some time, *you are not your failures.* No successful person has been launched directly from obscurity to notoriety, as if shot from a cannon. There have been years of planning, preparing, exploring, learning, failing, retrenching, relearning, and trying yet again. But most of all, such people had the courage to give whatever they wanted a whirl.

No successful person—successful, that is, at finding satisfaction in whatever one chooses for oneself—has blamed a parent for stopping her or him. Such people have often gone on despite parental wishes to the contrary. Perhaps they have given their parents the most precious gift of all, by thanking them and saying good-bye for now. If they are adults and emotionally freed from parental dictates, they can relate to others in a just way. They will require that what is asked and expected of them be available to them in return.

That is, if they are asked to be respectful, they will also want respect. Asked to demonstrate their love, they will expect that others will demonstrate theirs. Expected to gratify others' needs, they will expect reciprocity.

This is all part of being a grown-up—having the courage to be courteous to parents and getting what you want by changing your own behavior. Your parents have fulfilled their roles; you are now old enough to care about them in a mature way and go on with your life. You owe it to yourself.

Chapter Six

Mothers and Sons

Only a woman who has lived without romance knows how to value it. . . . That isn't true of my life either. I didn't live without romance. I found it . . . and I'm proud to have found it where you say it doesn't belong . . . in motherhood. I found it in my two [sons]. In Dave first and in Robin four years later.
—Sidney Howard, The Silver Cord

"My father," Garp wrote, "was a Goner. From my mother's point of view, that must have made him very attractive. No strings attached. . . ."
—John Irving, The World According to Garp

He sat down by the bed, miserably. [His mother] had a way of curling and lying on her side, like a child. The gray and brown hair was loose over her ear. . . .

His face was near hers. Her blue eyes smiled straight into his, like a girl's—warm, laughing with tender love. It made him pant with terror, agony and love.
—D. H. Lawrence, Sons and Lovers

As women, we have a great deal in common with all other women. Even if we meet a woman for whom we have little affection or affinity, still we understand her experiences with men and with her mother and father. We may not feel empathy with her, but we know whereof she speaks; we've been there too.

Our perspective on men, though, is foreshortened. To us they are almost alien beings—there is little with which we can identify. Or is there? Our differences with them appear to be more remarkable than our similarities. Their bodies don't seem to change as dramatically as ours during adolescence—they just get bigger. Most men grow up feeling entitled to the world's riches, and every last one of them, by virtue of his being a man, *does* have access to anything he desires, given ambition and perseverence. What we do understand about them is that they had parents, just as we did. And that relationship, especially with their mothers, is somewhat mystifying. It is she, after all, who gives a man his earliest image of womanhood.

Clearly, men are created too. They didn't just arrive on the scene possessing an inbred certainty that they control two lives—theirs and their wives'. Somewhere along the line, their personalities and philosophies were *shaped*. And this was a mother's work. The result of her influence is the man you see before you now.

Maybe you love him, but his contempt for women wreaks havoc with your life. You love him, but he won't allow you to make simple observations about his behavior, accusing you, instead, of attempting to emasculate him. You love him, but you can't remember the day he made a firm decision or took responsibility for his actions. You love him, but the prospect of forming a loyal bond with him appears doubtful—he's a perpetual womanizer. Who is he? What messages did his mother give him? What pains has he suffered? What, exactly, has his mother been to her son?

"My mother's fingerprints were very light on me. I felt she was never on my side—she was too involved with herself. To make my mother happy meant staying out of her way. She cared more for her peace and quiet than for me."

"I was about eight years old when I asked my mother if she believed in God. She told me it was a personal question and it was rude of me to ask."

"My mother was a liberated woman in the early 1920s. She believed in progressive education, woman's suffrage, and what was then called 'free love.' As to the last, she was horrified at the results—she had me. My father was married to another woman at the time. I grew up enormously disappointed and angry with her. She was eccentric and dotty and not what I'd ever call a proper parent."

"There was almost nothing I could do that would ruffle my mother. Being the only son with three sisters helped a lot. My mother was interested in anything I did, tolerated my moods, and wanted only my health and happiness. She was a very kind, Old World woman."

To understand the mother-son relationship, one needs to examine what the traditional marriage has meant for a woman—her very identity. Her world involved raising her progeny while she sought to keep her husband at her side. And she held to an unflagging belief in strictly divided marital roles. "To keep the man present and to preserve the nuclear family," George Gilder states in *Sexual Suicide,* "even love will not long suffice. He must be needed in a practical and material way." Men worked and were responsible for providing for their families and protecting the home. But that wasn't really all.

Because he spent so little time at home, a man expended just a small portion of his emotional side on his family. Fatigued from the pressures of his workday, a man often didn't want to be bothered with the minutiae of his wife's or his children's day. And if the children were to be disciplined—"We'll see what your father will do about *this!*"—they could be lined up and dealt with. Home was important, but less so to him than his job and what it meant to his masculine image.

It has been a common problem that a woman has experienced disappointment in marriage because she hasn't actually experienced her mate. During courtship, they probably shared excitement, interest, dreams. A man paid a lot of attention to his woman. After marriage, that attention often diminished to almost nothing. Seeing marriage as a trap, and his wife as his captor, he may not have withdrawn his physical presence, but he often denied his wife ongoing intimacy. So her disappointment took many forms. Her husband was not available to her because he was tired, and preferred hanging out with his friends on weekends. Their sex life was more agony than ecstasy; she was taken for granted, he no longer liked his "captor" and he may even have felt excluded from the family portrait except for the cash he contributed.

An interesting cycle starts when the husband is not emotionally accessible to the wife; she frequently turns to her children for comfort and connectedness. The negative messages received from her parents may still be resonating, so she becomes a woman full of doubts about herself. Her children, though, fulfill a need of which she may or may not be aware—that is, she desires intimacy and fears it at the same time. Married to a man who neither demands nor provides intimacy, she never has to confront this fear and come to grips with it. The son, then, provides a wonderful solace in the face of her fear. He is not going to *replace* her husband where physical intimacy is concerned, but he will allow her to construct a warm, safe relationship with a male who needs her.

Thinking herself a second-class citizen, she will not act upon her secret ambitions; if her husband fails to meet her needs in this area, she will direct her ambitions toward her son. A daughter is no help here—she'll grow up to be the same as her mother. A son, however, can conquer the world. This is the boy who will grow into a powerful man, do what she'd want to do if she were a man, be the complement to herself as a helpless, powerless female. A mighty ambition for her son, who eventually may not agree with her idea of his destiny. Yet, while she idealizes her son, cementing the bond between them, he is developing a sense of women.

Some mothers display great generosity of spirit toward other women—a fundamental trait for mothers. Others, as with every oppressed group, demonstrate a bit of self-hate, which is expressed in a rage toward those like them. As these mothers dislike themselves, so they also despise other women. Not aware of this tricky psychology as she forms her son's impressions not only of herself but of women in general, she raises a son who grows up disliking, fearing, or distrusting women. Such sons are often the men we marry.

What of the *healthy* mother? Such a woman tells her son

that women are to be loved, considered, and respected. Her advice to him is sensible; she tells him he will be better off with a woman similar to him in education, tastes, and style of living. Rationally, she will ask him to question the choice of a mate based on "chemistry"—which is often an attraction of opposites—rather than on the less explosive basis of compatability. A mother's demonstration of affection will show her son that, in fact, affection is natural, important, and not necessarily a prelude to sex. A good mother prepares her son to take care of someone else. She gives him a sense of worth, a clear idea of his place in the world—neither exalted nor debased. She will be instrumental, as well, in determining the nature and level of his ambitions. Finally, his understanding of a woman's desires and needs will come from her.

It is easy to be a healthy mother to a son, but you must be a healthy *woman* first. If you are not, you can come to hate him, clutch at him, haunt him, and bind him to you for the rest of your lives. No matter what he becomes, you'll be unable to cut your son loose to lead his own life. Why? You'll need him too much for your own affirmation. Any woman who's unhappy in her marriage because of an unavailable husband may think, *I'm not a man, I don't have a man, so I dare not lose my son. He's all I've got.* All mothers who are displeased with their lot in life perpetuate that displeasure by overprotecting and idealizing their sons. Much of this behavior is prompted by the mother's fear of losing her son, especially to another woman. To maintain the strength of her position, a mother may taunt her son with the purity of her love for him compared with the greedy, carnal desires of all other women who want him. In essence, she is saying, there will be no greater love than hers for him. In return for this love, she will not demand his body or his money, just his presence.

Wildly confused about his mother, a boy looks to his father for support and identification. If there is none forthcoming, he's caught. When a mother humiliates a father, the son can never want to be like him—and he certainly doesn't want to resemble his overbearing mother. How could he admire a woman who demeans his father? There are none of us so perfect that we don't say, "Look what dumb thing your father did today!" But this is episodic. If the denigration persists and forms a relationship that is characterized by emotional estrangement, the son can only hope to escape. Unless he *does* identify with his father, the son, in spite of himself, will resemble his mother, the true ruling force at home. He will then repeat the pattern by acting out with other women his conflicting feelings about being a male, to punish his mother while assuring himself that he isn't weak, like his father. As with daughters, there may be positional identification with the parent who holds the feared or envied position in the family. Like women, men become what they resist—in this case, their mothers.

MOTHER'S INFLUENCES

The frustrated mother may teach her son in a number of ways to dislike women. One way is by example. How does she react to his father's treatment of her? Does she simply accept the father's treatment, not out of sensitivity or awareness but out of submissiveness or helplessness? Is his father weak and his mother a tyrant? If the family unit is fragile, the son is well aware of it. If Mother points out that Father works hard, and this is the reason he can't always be there for his son, the son may feel a sense of loss or deprivation, but he'll realize that his father's absence has nothing to do with him. This is a normal response. If he hears instead, "You're father's nothing, a loser," she reinforces the belief that men don't meet women's needs.

When a father is neglectful or absent emotionally, a son doesn't learn to identify with him in a positive way; in fact, he doesn't want to identify with him at all. He often learns to manipulate the noninvolved father through the mother to get what he wants. (Son: "Dad won't let me go camping this weekend, and all my friends are going." Mother: "I know how to talk to him. You'll go.") Mother doesn't mind this collusion—her son, not her husband, comes first. He is the center of her universe. Soon the worshipful mother comes to dominate his life, and too late he sees what is going on. *He* is now the power in the family. This terrifies him. If Mother is a bit out of control with her love for her son, he may fear, during his adolescence, that she will approach him sexually. After all, here's Mom walking around unclothed, or consciously or unconsciously being seductive. At the same time, Mother is warning him away from girls: "We don't want a pregnancy, do we?" "Don't throw away your money on girls. You have better things to do with it."

"When my father left," a Denver man told me, "my mother barely let me out of her sight. I was eight years old then. A few years later an old boyfriend of hers returned to the city and they took up with each other. She made it utterly clear

148

that he'd never come between us. And he didn't. When I started dating, she didn't like it much. She could have a boyfriend, but I couldn't have a girl friend. Once my girl friend called in the evening, and my mother answered the phone. She told her I couldn't talk because I was doing my homework. Janet called back an hour later, and my mother said I couldn't talk because I was having dinner. She called back two hours later, and my mother said, 'It's too late to talk now!' and slammed down the phone. In all three cases, I was not doing what my mother said I was doing at the time. I found out about the phone calls from Janet the next day."

A man comes away from his worshipful mother with ambivalent feelings about her. He loves her but despises her; he seeks her comforting presence but fears her; he wants no woman who in any way reminds him of her, yet he's guilty because he can't be her "boyfriend" in the pure sense; he wants to be taken care of by other women the way Mother has taken care of him, but he also desires a woman whose caretaking is less emotionally strenuous. Mother, too, may be ambivalent. She wants her son to grow up, but she can handle him better if he's a little boy; she wants him to need her, but she fears that if he needs her too much, he won't grow up; she wants him to be a man who can make decisions, but she wants a strong voice in them; she knows he'll go on to other women, but she hates him for having sexual impulses that keep them apart.

Vivian is married to a man who was, and still is, the center of his mother's universe. When his mother calls, he jumps— enthusiastically and immediately. For the ten years of their marriage, Jack has compared Vivian unfavorably to his mother. Doubting herself, Vivian wonders if Jack isn't right;

maybe she is an inept housekeeper, an unimaginative cook, an ungrateful wife, a marginal mother. "My mother-in-law insists that Jack come over for lunch and dinner on Sundays, so he has at least 'two decent meals a week.' At my house, she thinks it's her privilege to open closets to see if the towels and sheets are stacked neatly and if the clothes are hanging by category—jackets with jackets, slacks with slacks, and so on. She even checks my kids' ears to see if they're clean! When I complain to my husband about what she's doing and ask him to talk to her about stopping it, he either denies that it's happening at all or says she doesn't mean anything by it."

Surprisingly, Jack insists that Vivian be passive in every way except sexually—she is to be aggressive and he is to be submissive.

When Vivian married Jack, she believed he was strong, loving, and affectionate. Most of all, she believed he would take care of her. Vivian soon discovered that he wanted her to take care of *him.* That was what his mother did for him and what he wanted from any woman he chose. While Jack fulfilled his mother's messages, Vivian fell unwittingly into a role she did not want. She cannot understand why he can't shake his mother's influence and be more sensitive to her needs.

Dr. James J. Rue and Louise Shanahan, in *Daddy's Girl, Mama's Boy,* said of the spoiled son's vision of relationships: "Any contrary expression [of adulation and affirmation] constitutes treason. Unfortunately, Mama has instilled this trait in him with such consummate skill that he does not realize the emotional problems he brings to marriage. . . . As an adult, he may interpret a relationship only in terms of what a woman can do for him sexually, never considering his responsibility."

Lorraine has her own story to tell of marriage to a man whose mother idolizes him. Demanding and rigid, Stan will not hear anything other than his own rules, needs, or opinions. If Lorraine does not behave in a way that pleases him, there is something amiss with her, he thinks. At no time does Stan consider that there is a way to behave other than his own, or that another valid point of view exists.

"There is one major conflict in our life—Stan's mother," Lorraine related. "About twice a year we visit his parents. We are not allowed to stay at a hotel, which I'd prefer, because his mother insists on having us at her house. The minute we arrive, the routine starts. I watch Stan turn into a child again. He takes his place as the baby of the family, and I swear, even his speech changes. His mother behaves as if a deity were levitating in her living room! And who am I? I'm the person with him. She can hardly get her mouth to form the word 'hello.'

"These visits are for Stan, and all I want to do is escape," she continued. "Stan, though, won't let me take the car and see some people I know. I'm supposed to sit on the couch and chat with his father while Stan and his mother coo over each other. Here's the worst part. Over dinner, Stan and his mother discuss whether or not I've been a good wife since the last time his parents saw me. While Stan's mother is around, I'm less than nothing."

It is Mother, after all, who is essentially responsible for whether or not her son will be a good lover and husband. By exploiting and manipulating him for her own good, Mother binds him to her so tightly that other women become interlopers, as in Stan's case. The mother who loves her son so fiercely presents a challenge to him almost on a daily basis: "Who do you love best? Her or me?"

Lorraine and Stan's story is not atypical. Ellen told me this about her husband: "Richard is aware of what his mother is doing to him, but he doesn't care to change it. Every morning, Richard's mother calls at six and says the same thing: 'Coffee's hot. Come on over.' So he leaves my side at six in the morning to see his mother before work. He stops off at her house after work, has something to eat there, then comes home to me and the kids. I'm upset over this arrangement, but I feel it would be cruel to say to him, 'Don't see your mother so often.' It would sound terrible.

"This is not all. On weekends, she always has a chore for him. It doesn't matter that Richard and I are about to go out for the evening. Once she called at seven on a Saturday night and asked Richard to come over and fix the furnace. She promised not to keep him long, but of course she did. The minute he got there, she had a three-course meal for him. I then got a call from him saying he'd be 'a little late.' I'm always competing with his mother for time and attention. I know I've lost."

Every good mother knows that when her son marries, his primary obligation is to his wife. Some mothers don't acknowledge it, and their sons may not want to change the order. Of course, a "mama's boy" loves the excitement his mother shows when he's around. He can do no wrong. He gets unconditional love, as if he were a nursing infant; few demands are made upon him, and the demands that *are* made are easily met. He receives excessive praise. In truth, running to Mother is a means of escaping his adult obligations to his wife, his life, even his job. Obligations at his mother's house, though, are minimal—he just needs to show up and he'll be coddled. Often, when a man gets older, he doesn't want this role of pampered babe, but he finds it difficult to extricate himself from it. His mother reminds him of all she's done for him. "Yes," mothers like these preach, "he has a wife, but a mother comes first. You can have a lot of wives," they press their point, "but only one mother."

As Mother rocked the cradle, she gave her son a variety of messages about himself, about women, about the world. It has been said that there are two predominating character formations in males—the aggressive, conquering type and the passive, dependent type—and that women bring up their sons to conform to one type or the other. In fact, most men fall somewhere between the two extremes, with something of each type in their makeup.

Freud once said that the favored son becomes the conqueror. This role is not without both problems and benefits. The favorite son may be provided by his mother with an inner strength—a drive, perhaps, to achieve. But the son who is favored and overwhelmed by his mother can also become an exaggeration of the conqueror—the macho figure who doubts his masculinity and therefore must subjugate women to prove that he's tougher than both his aggressive mother and his passive father. Such men are not interested in facing equals—women who will stand up for their rights, defy his injunctions, and ask that he consider their feelings.

153

He is interested only in women who worship the false image of himself his mother has given him.

The conqueror fulfills the ambitions his mother has not achieved or could not achieve; the passive, dependent son is bound to her in ways that her husband would not permit her to be bound to him; her son provides her with an emotional life. If the mother is in conflict sexually, she will transmit many of her conflicting impulses to her son. Either she will not give him any reasonable message about his sexuality, or she will diminish sexuality so he cannot perceive it as a normal, healthy process. Sex, she may warn, can stunt a man's growth psychologically or professionally. How? Because, she tells him, if you start caring about a woman, she'll make demands you can't meet.

Some men don't marry or marry late because of their mothers' unconditional admiration. The play *The Silver Cord,* by Sidney Howard, introduces a "professional" mother who was overbearing, who couldn't endure the loss of a son to another woman, who couldn't face her sons' sexuality or any of their other needs that fell outside her realm. Her eldest son, David, has married a woman who confronts her clutching mother-in-law, thereby severing connections between David and his mother. Panicked, she will not let her youngest son, Robert, who is engaged to be married, leave her. Fighting valiantly against the weaker Hester, Robert's fiancée, she wins her battle. Succumbing forever to his mother's "love" for him, Robert listens abjectly while she intones with near-religious conviction: "And you must remember what David, in his blindness, has forgotten. That mother love suffereth long and is kind; envieth not, is not puffed up, is not easily provoked; heareth all things; believeth all things; hopeth all things; endureth all things.... At least I think my love does?" Defeated, Robert replies, "Yes, Mother."

Some mothers may also take a less combative approach to women their sons bring home. This girl is too tall, that one too eccentric; this one is too outspoken, that girl's parents aren't "our kind of people." Others can't quite cope with a son's emerging sexuality and insult his choice of women.

"My mother had a mocking way with me about women," one Connecticut man confided. "First, she had nothing good to say about any girl I brought home. Second, she'd say something like 'Was that really *my* son with *that* girl?' as if I'd done something dishonorable by dating at all. I think she would have liked me to be a priest—a guarantee that I wouldn't have a woman."

The implacable mother's message to her son is clear: "Your choice of a woman isn't much, and neither are you. Should you marry her, I'll have to watch over her to make sure she's a good wife and mother." Should a son marry a woman of whom Mother disapproves, Mother may appear to groom her daughter-in-law to please her son, while providing just enough misinformation to assure that her boy will become unhappy and return to Mother.

The demonstration of a mother's ambitions through her son may have to do with his self-image—in spite of or because of his mother. She may tie him to her emotionally, only freeing him for a career, or she may force him to contain his ambitions by sabotaging them and making a nothing out of him. Here her power is at its most potent. Her son may say, "I want to go into real estate. I thought I'd take some courses." The mother replies, "You're making good money as a mechanic. When things don't work out, where will you be?" Stay with what you are now, this mother implores. Don't reach beyond that or test your capabilities. Don't prove that you can take risks and *win*. Be comfortable with less, and most of all, *need me*.

A mother who has an accusatory nature may twist a complaint she has about her husband, but dares not voice to him ("You don't take good care of me. You're cruel. You don't love me.") and direct a similar charge at her son ("You won't amount to anything. What do *you* have to offer a woman?"). As he grows up, the son internalizes his mother's insecurities, doubts, and frustrations. He may want to accomplish something, but he feels powerless in the face of her constant criticisms. Hating his mother, he's unable to tell her so. He can't bear the loss of whatever minimal affection she gives him, so he takes out his rage on the next woman in his life— his wife.

A woman who spoiled her son told me that he often boasted to her about his extramarital affairs. "I don't know what to tell him," she says, "how to answer. I don't want to be mean and tell him that he's hurting his wife and that he shouldn't do what he's doing. I feel sorry for my daughter-in-law, but who am I to tell him to stop?" I asked her why she doesn't advise him to remain faithful. "I think that what he's doing is terrible, but at least he tells me about it. He can trust me. But I won't tell him to stop. I don't want to lose my son."

Still giving her son unconditional love—no matter what he does or how it hurts others, it's all right—this mother accepts his behavior. She's always given him this kind of love, and he's still coming back to her to find it again and again with each new woman he takes up with. In many ways, he's bound to her. By talking about his other women, he's saying, "You're not the only woman, nor is my wife, who reminds me of you." But what he's implying is "I use these women for sex, but the woman I really love is you." He needs this kind of selfless caretaking from his mother, since his wife can't supply it. When his wife does something for him, this man may feel obliged to return the favor. His mother, though, doesn't ask for anything but his presence.

If a man never knows a loving, supportive, encouraging relationship from a mother who is willing to see him as someone separate from herself, who will allow him to step out into the world, who won't bind him to her to fulfill the emotional needs her husband can't meet, he will be in conflict about women. Afraid of tearing himself away from the object he depends on, a man such as this is a clinging child. If he's the "conqueror" son, he'll attempt to be powerful to prove his manhood. If he's passive, he'll search for a wife who's like his mother. With her, he needn't have a lusty, exciting relationship, but only remain a little boy and be taken care of—just as he was by Mother.

Now let's take a closer look at the effects a mother may have on the development of her son's personality.

TYPES OF MEN YOU MAY HAVE KNOWN

The "conqueror" typically needs constant praise and approval. He learned about uncritical love at his mother's knee. The conqueror's mother comes to his defense early on. (Teacher: "Your son struck another child on the playground." Mother: "He must have been provoked terribly, because my little boy would *never* do that.") She's not unlike the mother who pleads a son's case with "My son didn't murder seventeen people. They just stood in front of the gun when it went off." No matter what he's done, Mother is ready with an excuse for him. As he gets older, she pays his traffic tickets, fixes the car when he cracks it up, and keeps the information from his father. Most of all, she teaches him to place all blame on someone else: "Why were you staring at me? You made me drop the cup." "I only have sexual problems with you. I never had them with other women." "You told me to take that job and now I hate it. Why do I listen to a jerk like you?" "There's nothing wrong with the marriage. There's something wrong with your head."

The conqueror frequently cannot see beyond his own narrow point of view. If he doesn't have a feeling, experience, or opinion that coincides with his wife's—or anyone else's, for that matter—her feelings, experiences, and opinions are invalid. To him, other perspectives are unbelievable. His narcissism is complete; his idea of giving is lying back to be given *to*. The conqueror cannot look at himself and see faults—or acknowledge that he can be wrong, behave inappropriately, or be insensitive. Others erect obstacles in his life: "I do everything for my wife, but all she does is complain. Nothing is enough." "What do you mean, calm down! No one tells me what to do!"

This man will often become reckless—someone who tests the limits, because no limits have ever been set for him. He's emotionally brutal and exploitative toward women because he thinks women are there to serve him. When he wins, he tends to seize all the credit, but he shifts the blame for losses. This man often has grandiose ideas whose execution far exceeds his capabilities; perhaps he's the owner of a coffee shop who fancies himself a restaurateur of international renown. You may find him, though, passing much time in a local bar, bragging about his business acumen while standing everyone to drinks.

On the other hand, he's often very frightened to test himself, since he grew up with little or no responsibility. There's a part of him that knows he doesn't deserve all this uncritical acclaim he's gotten from Mother and is attempting to get from others. When he marries, he demands a submissive wife whom he torments with his directives.

And the passive man? Often, he is the youngest son in the family—the overprotected baby. Frightened of doing because he never did for himself, he secretly believes he has no ability to go out on his own. At the same time, Mother ensures that he doesn't learn to care for himself or make his own choices. He'll leave her, she fears, if he does. She prevents his growing into manhood by begrudging any praise or acknowledgment for any signs of masculine behavior. This is a man who learns he can get away with anything by being boyish or charming. He appeals to women's maternal instincts: "Do you know anything about sewing on buttons?" "Do you think you could cook for me someday? I'd really like that." He looks at women with beaming innocence, as if to say, "It's so nice being secure with you."

Appearing as a good-natured darling, or allowing a woman to have her way, is actually a coverup for his need to be done for. Flexible to a fault, he doesn't want to make decisions—what if they're the wrong ones? A strong woman is his preference. She can take control. He may even resent her for her control while being helpless to exercise the power. After a while she may not want to wield all the power, but to share it. A woman told me an example of her husband's indecisiveness. "Once my husband stopped in the middle of a street and started a traffic jam. He didn't know which way to turn, so he didn't. When I would offer no suggestions, he just stayed there!"

If a man appears devoted or submissive to his mother, beware—he's got a problem. He likes to have his mother around and may invite her to move in with him and his wife. Mother is only too happy to relocate. The passive man will always find someone just like his mother upon whom he can depend. The sexual side of such a man's marriage tends to deteriorate very quickly; to some degree, he can't perform sexually with his "mother." His sexuality thwarted, he may seek a woman outside the marriage, but more often the prospect scares him. And his wife, seeing him as a little boy, will also find sex with him problematic. He's a lover who may call out for direction, not as an attempt to please a woman, but more as a plea for approval and permission: "Am I doing this right?"

From the time he was a little boy, the passive man may have been told by his mother, "I sacrificed for you. I'm responsible for the fact that you're here." As a result, he may feel that he owes her, but how is he to repay such a debt?

Pitying himself, he gets what he wants by whining, complaining, and manipulating. He transforms his personality into a reflection of his mother's—the martyr, the self-sacrificer. He'll try every maneuver in his repertoire to get his way, including feigned illness, if that's what will work: "How could you go to night school and leave me to make my own dinner when I've got a splitting headache." "Oh, don't go out with your friends now. Stay home and keep me company." Whining and weak, he leans heavily on his wife, but satisfies his needs by adopting his mother's "feminine" wiles. Beware the weapons of the weak.

The passive, emotionally distant man is disturbingly unable to demonstrate affection. Appealingly self-assured, he presents himself as someone in control of his emotions, and he is. Suspicious of women, he fears that they will use him as he was used by his mother—for her own purposes. Women are for sexual pleasure, but he doesn't really experience much pleasure from sex. By setting up his life for him, Mother forced her own direction on him while remaining aloof to his desires. She inhibited his emotional growth by denying him warmth, love, and caresses. Now he cannot share these qualities with a woman.

Uneasy and withholding in emotional situations, he tends to experience deep depressions. Emotional issues are to be avoided. He is intellectually aware of his sadness, but emotionally he won't confront it. Though often attracted by demonstratively emotional women, he's scared, as well, that they may want him to reciprocate. "I love you" is a phrase that does not come easily to his lips, but he feels he can demonstrate love through financial generosity or just by being there: "Here's fifty bucks. Buy yourself a nice birthday present." "Do you need me to tell you you look pretty? Don't you look in the mirror?" He appears to be stable, calm, and in control, but it's the result of a monochromatic emotional palette. The woman who marries him must accept him as he is understanding that he doesn't have much more to offer.

And what of the bully? A man whose mother abandons him at an early age, or who neglects him, or is a brutalizer, shapes the eventually aggressive male. A user of women who appears to be the boyish sort, the bully is exploitative at the core—he's out to get what he can through strongarm tactics. Often he's the Don Juan who casts women off once they start to care. Violence is his hallmark; it's his answer to his mother's having left him—either physically or emotionally.

When Father leaves her, Mother, in her need to feel desirable, may abandon her son emotionally, perhaps devoting her energies to a series of lovers. Much intense sexual activity occurs in the mother's bedroom, and the son may hear or assume what's going on. Without the stabilizing model of sexuality within a setting of marital continuity and affection, the son, when grown, comes to use sex as a negotiating tool with women. Angry with his mother for continually testing her sexuality with men, he has difficulty in forgiving her for neglecting him and allowing anonymous men to use her. However, he's learned from his mother that partners are interchangeable. In his life, women will be the same to him as men were to his mother—one is as good as the next.

If mother gave him affection, perhaps it was inconsistent and meager. She may have been intense and loving one minute and brutal the next. He never knew what game she'd be playing next. Often an out-of-control female, she's confused about herself, and her son is caught in her web of hysteria. Attracted and repelled by women at the same time, he can be a cruel, deadly adversary. His pleasure, sexual and otherwise, springs from hurting women and exercising power over men.

Should the son of a sexually seductive mother be pampered between affairs and not be brutalized, the bully goes on to a fate similar to the son who was mistreated. Typically he has no emotional depth in relationships; with him, too, women are interchangeable. Often a sexual athlete, he's obsessed with giving pleasure—not for a woman's sake, but for his own ego gratification. One such man said to me, "I want a woman who has multiple orgasms because it gives me pleasure to please her." This is the classic myth the sexual bully believes in. The person who the world needs to move is *him*.

As stated earlier, the conqueror and the passive man do not exist in pure form. Though certain characteristics will tend to predominate, the opposite behavioral mode can emerge when certain events occur. The brutal man can, under severe stress, become the tragic, tearful, defeated man who needs tending. The self-effacing male can, in an emergency, perform heroic acts. As there are contradictions within men—within all of us—so there are contradictions in their relationships with the women in their lives.

Many men who did not have worshipful mothers are ambivalent about their mothers. They love them and despise them; see them clearly but are confused; wish they would conform more closely to an ideal image of womanhood but think they're fine as they are. They feel they know how to get Mother's approval, then wonder if they can ever please her at all.

One such man I know has a mother who's competent and

bright—a woman capable of earning an excellent income. When I first met Gary's mother, I thought he had a good relationship with her. Everyone who knew Gary and his mother believed the same of them. But what Gary told me proved that this was not quite the case.

"There was no real warmth," Gary said. "My mother rarely hugged or kissed me, but she performed her role as a good mother, or what she thought of as good—someone who took charge and made sure her sons were decent, wholesome, and hardworking. And we are, as it turns out. I love her, but I don't like her much. That's about it."

His wife told me of an experience that revealed Gary's mother's control over her sons and how it deeply affected her life. Toby said, "Two weeks after we were married and living in another state, Gary's parents came to visit us. His mother informed us that they would be staying with us, not at a hotel. I explained that we had only one bedroom. She said, 'We'll manage.' This meant that my in-laws got our bed while Gary and I slept apart for three weeks—me on the couch and Gary on a borrowed cot!

"Okay. Not only did his mother encroach on our territory by taking the bed—with Gary and me too intimidated by her to protest—she began decorating for us. She brought all sorts of dust-collectors—plates to hang on the wall, statuettes, and so on—that both of us hated. She did not care to hear our opinion about whether we liked it or not—what mattered was that she and my father-in-law agreed on where the junk should go. About twenty minutes after they left, I got pregnant.

"This was an enlightening experience for me," Toby added. "I'd always considered Gary's family an ideal one. I was mesmerized by his mother's formidable presence and concern for her family's welfare, and by his father's interest in his sons. But before this visit, I'd never realized how fully she treated her son, my husband, like a boy."

Gary, still under his mother's thumb, did not stand up for his or Toby's rights. He wanted his mother to "mother," to do what she'd always done—take over. But his resentment toward her remained unexpressed. Gary and Toby got a second chance to solve the problem, twelve years later. This time Gary's parents arrived hauling a large antique chest. "I gritted my teeth," Toby said, "and looked at Gary, who was rolling his eyes in annoyance. Finally I asked what the chest was for—certainly it was not for us. It was, naturally. I thanked my mother-in-law, but reminded her that since she hadn't thought twice about bringing it over without asking, and had assumed we'd be thrilled with it, she needn't think twice about taking it back. The price of that confrontation was ten years of silence. My in-laws wouldn't talk to us for an entire decade."

Standing up to a mother-in-law can be a paralyzing experience. But it can be done. It's not necessary to be rude or cruel to the mother of your husband, but it is important that she understand she can no longer control her son, or his wife through him. After all, if you thought enough of the man to marry him, she must have given him something you love. When her mother-in-law oversteps her boundaries, a woman's obligation to herself and her marriage is to confront her, with a husband's consent and affirmation. Your chances of establishing a position as an adult married to an adult are greater if you assert yourself when the problem first occurs.

In Toby's case, her mother-in-law reduced her newly married son and his wife to sexless children by seizing their bed. Both husband and wife, somewhat sexually innocent, still under parental influence, surrendered to the more powerful mother. Toby could see that the pattern of desexualizing her son had started when he was a child and continued with an attempt to separate him bodily from his wife.

SO, BEFORE MARRYING THE MAN . . .

If you look at the relationship between a man and his mother before marrying him, you'll get, if nothing else, a sense of how they treat each other. In describing these types of men in general, my intention is to make you aware of behavioral characteristics and how they evolve. So, before making a firm decision about a man, ask yourself these questions:

How does he describe his mother? How does he feel about her? Would he like to find someone like her? "My mother was passive, unmotivated," says one man. "My father took good care of her, but she was full of negativism. Nothing was good, no one worthy, and everything came in for criticism. I prefer women who are more vital, have interests and pursuits. I always felt my mother had no commitment to joy or happiness." What is he looking for in a wife? Do you want to make up to him for all the real or imagined horrors his mother perpetrated? Did his father abuse his mother? Did he think that was the correct way to handle a woman—through violence? If you are critical of him, can he take it? Does he strike back unmercifully because you dared to criticize him in some way? Does he always have to be right? Do you find yourself making excuses for him so he can be right? Is he reliable, dependable, and capable of interdependence? As one woman said of her husband: "He used to say that a good relationship was the most creative act a man could experience. He may have said it, but he's not around when I need him, is always late, switches appointments with our friends without telling me. If I'm feeling low, he tends to say, 'I don't know how to answer,' 'That's a real issue,' or 'What do you expect *me* to do?' So much for creative relationships."

In a good relationship, the role of the lover is interchangeable. Can you switch roles so one of you is in the foreground and the other in the background? Does he genuinely like women? Does he have to flirt with every woman in the room? Does he find the things you say interesting, or does he tune you out? Is he interested in you for content or packaging? Are looks of primary importance to him? Does he ask you to wear provocative clothes so he can show you off to other men? In effect, does he see you as a possession? Is he very conscious of the least wrinkle or gray hair you may develop, and remind you in a snide tone that you're aging? Is he hypochondriacal? Is every ache the first warning sign of cancer to him?

When you introduce a sensitive subject, does he develop a headache? Does he say "We'll talk about that some other time" on a regular basis? Does he fall asleep in your company because he's attempting to escape dealing with certain issues?

If you would like to make suggestions to him about how

he may improve his lovemaking, is he offended because he's had more experience and ostensibly knows more? Can he easily say, "I care about you . . . I love you"? In one woman's words, "My ex-husband said 'I love you' only three times in his life—once each to me, to his mother, and to our daughter. He always thought he was giving something up by using those words—as if he'd been born with a ration of 'I love you's' that could be depleted."

Does he regard displays of love as demands you place upon him? Does he think he'll explode into fragments of his former self, or lose something by giving? Can he laugh at himself? For example, can he go into a rage, then stop and say, "What am I doing? That's really not so important!" Does he tend to cry doom, believing that everything happens to him? Do you have to kiss his wounds? Do you always have to prop him up to send him out into the world?

Is this the kind of relationship that will endure? Is it the kind of relationship that has variety, a multitude of expressions of emotion and excitement, the potential of real intimacy?

Your answers to these questions will indicate whether a man is basically a person of some confidence and worth. If he's not, expect him not to allow you to be a competent person while pressing you to make him the main course. Not surprisingly, he'll be frightened lest anything you do might remove something crucial to his survival from him. Since so many relationships are structured so that there is room for one achiever only, you'll only make him appear less important if it's achievement you're after. If he, in his mind, appears less significant, he will sabotage your efforts to do more. For him to feel important, you must, by contrast, be unimportant.

Few relationships are ideal. Expecting a man to be everything, or to be there to provide emotional support all the time, is unrealistic. Ambivalence forms the core of most relationships—whether it's mother-and-son or husband-and-wife. It's impossible to be perfect. As for the man in your life, accept him as he is and you can help him build his strengths while understanding his weaknesses. Most of all, recognize that what you see is what you get.

Chapter Seven

Blurred Images

To "catch" a husband is an art; to "hold" him is a job—and one in which great competence is called for.
—*Simone de Beauvoir,* The Second Sex

It may be necessary simply to marry in order to find out what you don't want.
—*A. Alvarez,* Life After Marriage: An Anatomy of Divorce

Marry the man today
  Give him the girlish laughter
Give him your hand today
  And save the fist for after.
  —*Frank Loesser, "Marry the Man Today," from*
  Guys and Dolls

It has been said that self-improvement is the curse of the single woman, but it's certainly an improvement over a far more treacherous curse—"love at first sight." Motives for self-betterment usually have an authentic basis—you have a goal, you want to change your mode of life from not having to having. Not so dreadful a fate. The basis for love at first sight, though, is more obscure.

Shining with romantic glamour, this type of high-voltage meeting enthralls one or both of the parties involved. While all others are dim shadows by comparison, the instantly perceived beloved is incandescent—a powerful presence. Popular romantic literature describes the "love at first sight" scenario as an engulfing experience—his hypnotic gaze, her quickening body, his wolfish grin, her fluttering heart, his electric touch, her knowledge that "this is the man for her." The encounter, thus far, has consumed approximately thirty seconds of two lives. He has not yet heard her last name spoken aloud, nor has he a clue to what she wants from life; she only knows he's not a maniac out to do her wrong, but could it be? Is he her *salvation*?

Because emotions can grip us so strongly in so short a time, those smitten by an infatuation naturally suppose that whichever feelings gush to the surface are significant, genuine, and definitive. They *are* significant—genuine, too—but definitive they are not. If anything, love at first sight demonstrates an *illusion* about love, and is not a true test of connectedness. Despite its feverish symptoms, love at first sight is not necessarily truth. Rather, it implies that you've taken an unknown (the beloved) and transformed him into a known ("intuitively" and unquestionably, he's for you), without going through the process of knowing (sharing experiences together). On what, truly, is this kind of love based?

Were you to examine the person with whom you've fallen in love, you might discover that he's the embodiment of a fantasy, a close-enough duplicate of a lost love, a man who physically, or by attitude or inflection, reminds you of someone from the past. He could be a dynamic figure you want to love, if not forever, then for a night; after that night, he may be someone you will want forever. But this scenario, too, is grounded in illusion. Celia's story exemplifies the trap concealed in love at first sight.

On an early-morning flight from New York to Los Angeles on business, Celia, a fashion buyer, decided to curl up and take a nap. When she awoke, she found a bottle of champagne tucked under her arm. Celia called over the stewardess to ask the identity of the mystery donor. She was told that the man in question would make himself known to her at the baggage claim in Los Angeles.

"I was terribly flattered," Celia related, "and couldn't guess who'd been this flamboyantly generous. When I got to the baggage claim I was pretty keyed up. No one said a word to me until I pulled my suitcase from the carousel. Then a voice came from behind me and said, 'I'll take that for you!' I turned and faced a distinguished, richly dressed businessman. He smiled seductively. 'The champagne . . .' he said, trailing off, as if no more need be explained. I thanked him, already attracted to him. He asked where I'd be staying, and offered me a lift. I accepted.

"I expected a cab ride from the airport, but a limo was waiting at the curb; it was his. We exchanged introductions and he presented me with his business card. I'd heard of him. We chatted in the backseat of the car for about fifteen minutes when he suddenly suggested that I come with him to his hotel and unpack what I needed for the night. Then he'd have his driver take me to my hotel to check in. He squeezed my hand and looked imploringly into my eyes. He was forward, too confident, but persuasive. I was hooked. Without a fuss, I agreed.

"At his hotel, he gave me a quick kiss," Celia recalled,

173

"and said, 'Let's have dinner at seven-thirty. We'll decide where later.' On the way to the hotel, I wondered what I'd gotten into, wondered why I'd so passively gone along with him, but mostly wondered how often I'd get to see him. One night? Two? It didn't matter right then. This was high adventure to me—maybe even more than that.

"I went to a late-afternoon business meeting and could barely concentrate on what I was doing. The man's effect on me was disturbing. Within a few hours I'd been reduced to a mooning adolescent. I'd mindlessly followed a man, a perfect stranger I trusted only because of his position, and with whom I'd agreed, nine hours in advance, to spend the night. He'd charmed me, overwhelmed me, told me what I must do to please him, and, as though hypnotized, I did as I was bidden.

"Dinner was to be at his hotel. He said it would be easier that way, and asked me to pick him up at his room. All right, I thought, one hotel dining room is as good as the next. This one's just closer to his bed. Then something scared me. As I dressed, I realized my fear was not of going to bed with him but that, upon seeing me this evening, he'd change his mind about my desirability.

"An hour later, my hand trembling," Celia continued, "I knocked at his door. He opened it and stood before me, wearing a boyish smile. A damp towel was wrapped around his waist. Was he going to tear it off and lunge at me? He couldn't be that crude. He explained that he was running late and told me to fix myself a drink while he dressed. How *could* I have doubted him! Then there was a knock at the door; he called to me from the dressing room to answer it; it

174

was room service. Interesting, I thought, he ordered dinner in his room. I was beginning to piece a few items together— mostly based on speculation. He was probably married and couldn't be seen with a woman in public places, restaurants included. At least that was what I chose to think. This room was to be his sanctuary, and mine, as long as I didn't answer the phone or make a scene. That was fine with me. I, and no other woman, was the chosen one.

" 'You're beautiful,' he said to me when he exited from the dressing room. He was casually dressed; I was overdressed. I didn't much care, nor did he, apparently. What I cared about was him—I felt I was in love."

Celia could barely choke down dinner, waiting for the inevitable to happen. When he finally touched her, she experienced a great loss of control, even as another part of her fought to counter it. "It was almost as if I were two selves." One self was grappling to maintain a semblance of sanity— the self that knew if I let go emotionally with this man, I'd find recovery painful when he left me. The other self was filled with reckless desire and didn't much care what my rational self was preaching about self-preservation.

"Over the next three days," she said, "my wardrobe, piece by piece, wound up in his closet. On the morning of the fourth day, he kissed me good-bye as usual and wished me a profitable day. I returned the good wishes. I had a noon meeting, and that was it. I returned to his room at three, called my hotel for messages, and decided to take a shower. I opened the closet to get my robe, and found it empty of his things. I raced to the bathroom; nothing of his remained. Trembling, I called the desk. He'd checked out, the desk clerk informed me, and paid the bill, and could I please, by the way, be out of the room by four o'clock? Had he left a message for me? He had not, the clerk replied. I tore through every drawer, searched my luggage, pulled back the blankets—he had to have left a note somewhere! Nothing. "What could I do? I let out a scream of despair and collapsed. I'd been a complete fool. I'd loved him from the first night and he probably knew it. Finally I got my bearings, gathered my belongings, and dropped the champagne cork I'd saved as a memento into the trash basket. I thought I'd die if I never saw him again, and that I'd want to kill him if I did."

So, as mysteriously as he had entered Celia's life, he disappeared. Celia "fell in love" with a practiced rake, the way many of us fall for men with a lot less flair who are nonetheless equally as enticing. What is love all about, then?

Falling in love is not as sudden an occurrence as the hypnotic locking of glances across a room, the exchange of a few charming comments, or the passage of an evening—or two or three nights—together. For a woman, physical penetration is not the ultimate act; a man penetrates her psychologically, as well. A brief encounter may seem to be made more meaningful if one calls it love, but if there is no real love, it is only sexual sport.

Falling in love is a gradual process that starts with two strangers encountering each other; then each learns who the other is. At some point, both parties decide that each enhances the life of the other; there is a continual bonding and a sense of profound love that can be recaptured, in one's reverie, when the other isn't around. True love reveals a genuine empathy for another person; this is a quality that cannot develop unless there is maturity—unless each can see the world from the other's point of view, while recognizing that sexual experiences heighten and deepen the bond. There is desire and preference for the other, although each can live alone. For some women, it would seem, love is a dream, an irretrievable passion from the past; possibly it brings security or adventure, or verifies an ill-defined theory of the purpose that love is intended to serve.

These blurred images of love come from a diffuse or disorderly picture of intimacy. There is little understanding in such images of the sequence of getting to know a man, liking him, becoming intimate with him, and deciding whether the relationship will endure or not. Romantics, who believe the image of love is clear—though it is not—throw themselves into relationships. Often they are emotionally chaotic people; there is little order to their lives, or they live otherwise structured lives but are vulnerable because a crisis has thrown them off balance. In a misguided attempt to regain equilibrium, they opt for fantasy, that breathless romanticism. But this is neither a reasonable nor a healthy approach to life, with love as a filler, replacement, or palliative. "He who marries from love must live in sorrow," a Spanish proverb says, though many women with romantic inclinations would doubt this seeming cynicism. Love may be a blurred image, they think, but it's better than not loving at all.

In an attempt to court love when it doesn't court them, many women pursue men. The rules of the dating game have changed over the last fifteen years—it's okay, some feminists insist, to call up a man and ask him out before he asks you. I disagree with this. It is right that the male pursue the female, and for several reasons: by taking the initiative, a

177

man shows his willingness to extend himself a bit more. It also means that when there is love, he may love you more than you love him. When women pursue, they set up a situation that never gives a man a chance. He can't go that extra inch, since he wasn't trusted to do it in the first place. And should you marry the man you pursue, you must expect to sustain that pursuit during marriage. While his feet are up on the coffee table, a deaf ear turned to you, he will still be unattainable while you are chasing after his affections. If you give of yourself extravagantly to get him, he will expect it of you for the duration of your marriage. Allow yourself to be pursued, and he will be able to take charge, make plans, make an effort to please you. He may not be as attentive in marriage as he was in courtship, but he will still hold on to the role of the pursuer. When he courts you, he's interested in knowing what you require of him. If he wants you enough, he will find a way to get you.

Second, it is right that he should desire you sexually. That his desire equal yours or be a little greater than yours is crucial, for him, physiologically, as regards his ability to fulfill his role. It is easier for a woman to be with a man whose desire for her is greater than hers is for him. In the opposite situation, it may be difficult for him to acquire or sustain an erection, whether his sexual drive is high or low. Any woman can lie there pleasantly—and I don't mean this harshly—which has more to do with her wanting to be close to or please a man. Since a man must function physiologically for a satisfactory sexual experience, he cannot lie there pleasantly; he cannot be passive. If they don't experience ejaculation, most men feel a sense of loss, a physiological and psychological strain.

COMMUNICATION: GETTING THROUGH TO HIM

Freud considered sex and anger the two pivotal drives in human beings; guilt, jealousy, depression, fear, and sexual dysfunction all derive in some way from these two basic drives. Sex is often used as a problem-solving device in a relationship—a way to discharge unpleasant feelings, cover them over, or avoid them entirely. Most often, sex cannot help us get to the core of a problem, but anger can.

Many of us can't handle anger. A fit of temper can frighten us so that we either repress it ("No, I'm not angry that Burt left me. I expected it! Let her have him, that jerk!"), blame our unhappiness on fate or on other people and live in a state of perpetual discontent ("Life is such misery . . ."), or connect anger, incorrectly, with violence ("If I get mad, I'll lose control and kill him."). Anger is actually a form of communication—a method of telling another person how you feel. Its purpose is not to destroy that person but to put an end to the destructive acts that are hurting you. Simply, anger is an assault on the act, not on the person.

Anger is a positive emotion when it is discharged to rectify problems, not when it is used to aggravate those problems or to put off their resolutions. The truth is, when you get angry, you really care. So, when you concern yourself with how you care, and not with how angry you are, anger itself will be constructive. All too many of us would admit to days of unproductive shouting at a spouse. But, if friendship exists between a couple, each wants good things for the other; to get those good things, strategy and compromise must be learned, and anger can help to express the truth.

If you get the anger out when you begin to feel it, you won't have to be afraid of the consequences. Women often have difficulty expressing anger, and carry old injustices around with them for years: "Why didn't you tell me sooner that we're not going to the movies? It's so like you to make me unhappy . . . like the time you cancelled our trip to the Poconos . . . and the leather coat you promised me three years ago." When you don't discharge anger, it follows that you can't bear making love to the man who has enraged you. You think he's an insensitive fool, a torturer. You perceive him as a man who possesses only negative attributes, and therefore you can't feel kindly and loving toward him.

We have trouble letting go because we're not practiced in being angry. We're specialists at shouting and having tantrums, but not at exercising *productive* anger. Some women come from homes where no important issue was ever resolved. As a result, such women have become shrill, short-tempered screamers, or have repressed their anger entirely, out of terror. Women feel guilty about expressing anger and don't know what to do with it. Men, when they're angry, can often cope with the feeling, but may not be able to come to a resolution without the cooperation of a woman who seeks one. After a confrontation, men often want to make up. We don't appreciate that. Since we haven't fully discharged our feelings, and they have, we're angrier when they suggest sex as the next step. And we hate that. Men often lack expertise in expressing themselves emotionally in ways we can appreciate. It's difficult for them to say, "I'm sorry," and even more of a chore for them to say, "I was wrong."

Men, asking for sex after an argument, don't really see themselves as "using" us. They don't know any way of saying, "Let's get close again," except to say, "Let's go to bed." Still angry, we assume we are to be the receptacle for his passion. What's wrong with that? Are they damned if they do and damned if they don't? But if you are still angry and don't want to submit, acknowledge it. Without attacking him or his sexuality, without bringing up a grievance that happened ten years before, tell him what bothers you. Remember, anger has a purpose; it allows you to change behavior. If you injure someone you love through continued personal assault, love will suffer. Blowups are natural in a relationship, but if you care about each other, there's nothing that can't be worked through when you both cool down a bit.

I want to emphasize a point here about men and communication. We believe that men never think about us, but that we think about them all the time. This is not true. They just think about us in a manner that's unfamiliar to us. Though we all speak the same mother tongue, we do not necessarily use the same words. Men are vaguer in describing their emotions. Often, in the business world and among friends, men communicate in the jargon usually reserved for combat or the ballfield. We may want them to gush like those heroes with sardonic grins in romance novels or movies, but few have the resources to carry it out. This is a fact of life. And because we don't know what they mean, we can only doubt them. Then again, they may not understand us if we are circuitous, manipulative, or suggestive.

You may prefer volleying terms of endearment, and he may be exhausted after tossing out one such as "I like you a lot." Still, you can achieve a level of communication. One way is to soften your vocabularies so they are in a "comfort zone" for both of you. Women tend to overwhelm and frighten men with their language. And while we may be able to cheer them, flatter them, and reassure them in language they need to hear and respond to, they don't necessarily have the ability to reciprocate or even to express anything more than what we take to be grudging compliments.

A man who has difficulty in expressing his feelings needs gentle, persuasive coaching. Though he knows what needs to be said, he may not care to say it. He believes you want effusive flattery, and perhaps you do. He believes you want acknowledgment of what you've done for him, and you certainly do. But you have to listen hard to catch his drift. When we don't get that compliment, we may attack with cracks like "Would it kill you to say I look nice?" Without looking at you, he may say it, which then may inspire a sarcastic rejoinder from you like "That wasn't hard, was it?" This is an instance of two people playing two different games at the same time. In effect, you are punishing him for complimenting you.

When you tell a man what you want to hear by expressing it clearly, he will understand: "It would please me if you'd tell me that I look nice." This will get his attention. Let's go another step. Suppose a woman is anxious to see a man more often. How does she get him to call her? Not by reacting in the following manner when he does call: "Oh, you didn't have anything better to do but call me? What happened? No buddy to see tonight?"

Let's look at a specific case. Marcia is committed to Ken and would marry him tomorrow; he is doubtful about her and has said little about their future—though he does tantalize her by talking of possibilities. Ken calls Marcia for a Saturday-night date. Wanting to make him jealous, Marcia has accepted a date with another man. "Sorry, I'm busy," Marcia tells him, then pauses a moment and adds, self-destructively, "but where would you have taken me?" Ken replies quickly, "You're not breaking a date to see me." This puts Marcia on the defensive. "I don't intend to," she says. Both of them know she would have, since she's done so in the past. Why ask what Ken had planned? She's made both of them uncomfortable. All she had to say was, "Sorry. I'd love to see you another time." But Marcia doesn't stop there. "I'm not doing anything on Sunday," she croons. "I am," Ken replies, allowing Marcia to infer the rest: *And I'm not inviting you.*

As with Marcia, many of us tend to be too wildly impulsive, too accessible, too intent on tricking men into giving us what we want. In reality, Marcia suffers more by knowing what she has missed by accepting a date with another man by not being available than by being too available. Then Ken doesn't want her. Marcia would like to have it all, but she can't. She made her choice. She has not yet learned when to speak, when to hold back, when to give.

Marcia's failing is that she thinks in extreme or catastrophic terms. If someone's response to her is "That's nice," it's not only not good enough, but borders on insult. "You're spectacular . . . the meal was heaven . . . I had an incredibly great time" are statements more in keeping with what she considers her due. Marcia wants ovations, adoration, honeyed words. When they are not forthcoming, "the evening was a disaster," she's "doomed," her life is "shattered." She's not unlike the confused, boy-crazy heroine of Ring Lardner's perfect profile of the catastrophizing female in his story "I Can't Breathe." While having fun juggling three men and concealing her contempt for them, Lardner's heroine declares to her diary with world-weary exasperation: "I know I'll never live through the night. . . . I can't stand it, I can't breathe, life is impossible. . . . I simply mustn't think about it or I'll die. . . . A whole year and [Merle] still cares and I still care. That shows we were always intended for each other and no one else. I won't make *him* wait until December. . . . And when I get home Sunday and Walter and Gordon call me up, I will invite them both to dinner and Merle can tell them himself [about the wedding], with two of them there it will only hurt each one half as much as if they were alone. . . . I can't stand it."

Marcia could change her life if she changed her vocabulary. There are gradations of positive feeling—one thing may be pleasing, another displeasing; there are moments of comfort and discomfort: Life does not consist of extremes of pleasure or pain. There is a wide middle ground that is not characterized by drama, cataclysm, or breathlessness. Women like Marcia do not accept less than immoderate praise, and feel that they must be wildly enthusiastic or severely depressed to persuade others that their feelings are genuine. "Nice" is a compliment, not a snub. So if a man is the sort who can only summon "Nice," give him the "Thank you" he deserves.

CONFUSIONS IN LOVE

"Humans are never so vulnerable as immediately following orgasm," James Ramey states in *Intimate Friendships*. And, he continues, "This is a major reason why many people use sexual intimacy as an avenue to establishing intimate friendships—because it is a 'shortcut' to making one's self vulnerable—and it is this willingness to be vulnerable to the partner that promotes the sharing of intimacy and love."

These shortcuts to intimacy and love often fall wide of the mark. Sexual intimacy is just that—an amusement for a few hours, maybe for the duration of the night. The man will not be there tomorrow; you might not even want him there and hurry him out. These encounters, one-nighters, are dilemmas to some women who submit to them and then want to win affection. It doesn't seem to work.

Why do they leap into bed with men they've known only for an hour or two? Following rejection by a husband or a long-term lover, rebounding from an affair, or suffering the trauma of reentry into the singles' world after a divorce, a woman may feel that life is not going well and she needs affirmation of her desirability. Or perhaps life is going quite well but she has no one to share it with. Or perhaps a handsome stranger says he must have her and she feels she might never have a chance like this again. All of these are possible motives for instant intimacy. Sexual giving does not guarantee love—or even so much as a promise of future meetings. If both parties know that each will supply the other with a few hours of warm human contact, it may be bearable to a woman when her lover leaves her bed. Even then, women tell me, there is a ponderous sadness, a feeling of emptiness. He may have been a "hit and run" type, she might have thrown herself under the wheels, so to speak, but she thought she was invulnerable because she consented. Not so. Many of us will still wonder why he didn't call, though we know, as one woman put it, "if he did, we wouldn't have had much to talk about anyway." In the matter of one-night stands, she continues, "We have no one to blame but ourselves. Instinctively we know that a man is totally inappropriate for us, and often wonder how we managed to chat as much as we did before getting into bed. In my experience, I've had nothing in common with men I've only wanted for bodily contact, except that we were at the same party."

Not all intimate moments with a "stranger" are limited to one-night stands. Established relationships wherein one party is emotionally estranged from the other can be as unfulfilling, and far more painful. Let me tell you about Patty. Twenty-six and divorced, Patty is dating a man to whom she is a sexual slave. Her relationship with him has followed the same pattern for the last year. Rob returns home from a date at one or two in the morning, then calls Patty to come over to his place for a romp. She agrees. Patty pulls herself out of bed, drives a few miles to his house, disrobes, has sex with him, then gets up at five in the morning to go back home because "he doesn't like anyone there when he gets up." Less time is devoted to communicating and caring than to sex before both drop off to sleep.

Patty will tell you she's "crazy" about Rob, obsessed with him, but when I met her, I saw a woman whose self-esteem was so low that she was perilously close to suicide. As if Rob's late-night summonses aren't destructive enough, Patty does herself further damage by spending her weekends driving past his apartment to check whether the lights are on and his car is parked in front of the building; this usually means another woman is there with him. Given a choice, Patty would not want to break up with Rob but have his baby. Her rationale is sadly childlike: "I'll have something of his that he can never have, see, or touch. I could maybe get myself not to want him anymore, but I want his child!"

Since Rob has made it clear that sex is the only area in which she brings him gratification, Patty mistakenly believes she can extend that gratification to other areas. Rob, only too happy to summon her when he wants her, has no interest in knowing who she is. Nor does he care about her well-being. Never does he escort her from her car in the middle of the night; neither will he suggest that she call him to let him know she's arrived home safely. As long as she jumps when she's beckoned, he'll call her.

Patty is not the first woman to be obsessed with a man whose interest in her is negligible. He has a quality she needs to sustain not her good feelings about herself but her insecurities. Patty is addicted to him—no other man can make her feel quite as good, desirable, vital, when he's with her. Without him, she suffers from "withdrawal" symptoms; she's depressed, panicked, unable to concentrate. Every cup of coffee reminds her of one she took with him—in that dim past when he actually took her out before taking her to bed. Yet, since she's nothing to him, he treats her like nothing and discards her after he's taken his pleasure.

Stanton Peele, who has written extensively on addiction, says in *Love and Addiction,* written with Archie Brodsky, "An addiction exists when a person's attachment to a sensation, an object, or another person is such as to lessen his appreciation of an ability to deal with other things in his environment, or himself, so that he has become increasingly dependent on that experience as his only source of gratification." And love, he continues later on, "is the opposite of interpersonal addiction. A love relationship is based on a desire to grow and expand oneself through living, and a desire for one's partner to do the same thing."

In marriage, a partner's obsession or addiction may focus less on the other person than on an *act.* Married for thirteen years, Arthur and Jeanne are a prime example of misplaced "loving." They met when they were very young; both were from bitterly unhappy homes. Arthur was the youngest of five children; his mother abandoned the family when he was a baby. Jeanne took fourth place in a home with three older brothers who were given all the encouragement, emotional support, and whatever money there was for education. Arthur and Jeanne found identification with each other based on their unfortunate childhoods—that is, they understood each other's pain. Arthur, a blue-collar worker, is bright and marginally ambitious; Jeanne, until a few years ago, stayed home to tend to the house and raise their two children.

When the children were both in school, Jeanne decided to get a realtor's license. As she began to succeed in her new endeavor, Arthur became unnerved, threatened. Jeanne wanted her job, but she needed Arthur to help raise the children—he was a good father, and she appreciated this in him. Jeanne couldn't bear the thought of being a single parent. Full of insecurities from her past, Jeanne couldn't move, either further into the marriage or out of it. She needed the stability her marriage gave her. Arthur didn't see other women, gamble, or drink, and he had an admirable set of traditional values. Their problem, though, was that Arthur was unrelentingly sexual, and demanded that Jeanne submit to him nightly. This would have been fine if Jeanne were as sexual as Arthur; but she was not.

After each sexual episode, Jeanne was reduced to tears. Arthur was known to pull her legs apart to have oral sex with her; the act offended her. Jeanne couldn't abide Arthur's sexual demands, and over the years she stopped loving him. Arthur would deny that he was essentially raping his wife. To him, he was communicating his need for her in the only way he knew how. Jeanne, a woman who didn't relate primarily through sex, was despondent.

To Arthur, sex was the only way to please her and, more important, to keep her close. Underneath it all, the thought of losing his wife panicked him. He didn't want to look for sex outside the marriage; he thought infidelity was morally wrong, but that raping his wife was not. Arthur knew Jeanne didn't love him, but he was also aware of her conflict about leaving him. As long as she was with him, he was content.

When I saw Jeanne and listened to her story, I asked how she thought a resolution could be effected. She despaired of finding one; sex had become abhorrent to her. How many times a week, I asked, could she tolerate sex. Twice, she answered. I suggested she speak to Arthur and find out how many times a week he really needed sex. She reported back: twice. Jeanne then picked the days they'd have sex—Wednesday and Sunday—and sealed an agreement with him that there would be no variation from this schedule. Then Arthur again demanded sex on his terms. "He made a deal with me," she said, "and now he wanted to break it. A year ago, I'd have just gone along with it. Now I just refused. When he wanted sex every day, I thought it was because he desperately needed it. When he told me twice a week was good enough, I was surprised—and angry."

Like Arthur, many men have little experience with women wanting them sexually, and don't know how to motivate desire in a woman. Frequently such men do not recognize when wives—or other women, for that matter—come on to them sexually. They see women as just being "charming" or "friendly," but do not see the reason for the charm or friendliness as having anything to do with them. Essentially, they are little boys who have scant experience, other than with their wives. And since such a man's wife is *his,* she's supposed to want him; in fact, she'd *better* want him. Others, to demonstrate their control, have never *made love* to their wives, but force their attentions on them. These wives wouldn't know what it's like to be made love to—they just know what it's like to have sex. Sexual encounters are, then, a display of aggression, not passion, a power struggle wherein sex is used to overwhelm a woman, rather than to express mutual attraction or passion.

DEALING WITH SEXUALITY

A friend told me this story. Years ago, she attended a party, given by a wealthy businessman, alone. When it was time for her to go, the host escorted her to her car and kissed her sweetly. Andrea reported that she was both flattered and irritated by the kiss—she appreciated the gesture but believed it was a game for him. Her look of surprise did not catch him off guard; he was experienced enough to sense her unspoken thoughts: *Do you do this with every woman? Am I just the woman of the moment?* He said quickly, "No matter what experiences we have in life, each connection is unique. These four lips have never touched before."

She laughed and realized the truth; it was just an innocently sexual, affectionate gesture that merely acknowledged his interest in her, although he had no intention of going further. Like my friend, we often feel put upon, and reflexively recall our past experiences or worry about the future: *What does he want? What does this mean?* Unfortunately, we don't appreciate the unique sexual interaction of any two people at any given moment. Locked into her restrictive sexual script, Andrea was prepared to fend off a pass from a man she believed would proposition her.

For one to express sexuality fully and pleasurably, it is necessary first to relax, make a connection with one's body, and disconnect the old messages about sex being forbidden, a chore, a means to control a mate. Then there will be not only orgasm but the pleasure of mutual exploration. Women who have been taught that sex is disgusting, or acceptable only when procreation is desired, must then make the transition to another level. Such a woman's husband may not want a woman who merely tolerates sex because he may consider her lack of responsiveness demeaning to him; this type of man desires a woman who likes sex, is proficient at it, and can have an orgasm. Sexual enthusiasm is difficult for some women; it takes time, devoted effort, and a willingness to accept one's own sexuality in order to learn to enjoy sex. Attitudes about sex *can* be changed.

Sex is the only drive that is thwarted, under "normal" circumstances. If you're hungry, you'll eat, and if you're thirsty, you'll drink. Sex, which is not fundamental to immediate survival—you can live without sex, as any monk content in his celibacy will affirm, but not without bread—is easily channeled into other activities. Working, tending children, cleaning house compulsively, even overeating, are a few examples. One's sex drive can be stemmed by ceasing to pay it attention at all or by calling it something else. Not unlike the anorexic who thwarts the drive to eat, the sexual thwarter is still preoccupied with what she is denying herself.

Sex may be made into an enigma ("I don't know what I'm supposed to feel or how to feel it."); a project to be directed by a taskmaster ("Let's see if you can have an orgasm tonight or not."); or a competition ("I'm a lot more sexual than you are."). We create complications by not perceiving sex as a nice, easy, fun-filled, and warm extension of intimacy. Instead, men will issue orders—as will some women—coercing their partners to "do it my way and no other." In one extreme case I know of, a husband would slap his wife across the face if she dared move during the sex act. As part of this man's upbringing, he had been taught that women weren't supposed to like sex, cooperate with it, or demonstrate passion during it. If she became even marginally excited or—heaven forbid—sexually abandoned, it meant to him that any other man could take his place. For the sake of his fragile male ego, women were to lie there motionless and merely receive: They were not to participate and give.

Conversely, there are women who are reticent about expressing their sexual needs, fearful that they will offend their husbands or embarrass themselves by talking about what they prefer. "If he cared about me, he'd know what I want by now" is the common complaint. However, if a woman never tells a man what *does* please her, and he hasn't thought to do it in the past, how will he know?

There are also women who would happily exchange places with the aforementioned unresponsive wife—though most would just as gladly do without the penalty for sexual movements. They would be content simply to lie there while the deed is done to them. Such women often do participate more actively in sex, but not because they crave intimacy or the sharing of an inspired moment of passion. Rather, they engage in an activity distasteful to them because there will be a payoff. After sex, they will mention the earrings they saw today, the car they want for Christmas, or, as one woman put it to her husband, "Now can I have a new living room suite?" Unable or unwilling to make an emotional connection with their husbands, such women detach themselves from the sexual experience and perform mechanically while they are spiritually elsewhere.

Yet, while tuning out their husbands, it is not uncommon for a notable number of married women to tune in to another man. See if the following tale sounds familiar. A married woman, not especially searching for a lover, serendipitously finds a man who'd like to play the extramarital game. She considers the risks, the excitement, the end of boredom at home. "Why not?" says she. Her intended lover calls her on a Monday, sure that her husband is off at work, and after a few delicious compliments to her, suggests they meet at the No-Name Motel at two o'clock on Thursday. For the next three days she's in a heavenly haze of fantasy about this meeting. She prepares herself the way she once prepared herself for her husband—she stocks up on a few daring items of lingerie, gets a facial, scrutinizes her body to see what can be done to make it look better in seventy-two hours. By the time she gets to the motel room, her clothes are practically off already and she's breathless from needing her lover.

Now suppose this woman has no lover, no opportunity to take up with one, or no inclination to go outside her marriage for sex. Her husband calls her one afternoon and asks that she send the kids to her mother's for the evening and that they share a romantic, lusty evening alone. Shrilly she replies, "Are you kidding? I have too much to do. Bobby has the sniffles ... I promised Rosalie I'd help her hem her drapes ... I don't feel like getting done up in this weather, and how *could* you be so selfish!" The rejected husband swallows the insult and his pride, and a few months later gives it another try. He calls at eleven o'clock in the morning and says, "I have a slow afternoon. Why don't I come home for lunch—a nice late lunch." No more need be said. The uninterested wife responds, "How do I know what I'll be doing in an hour? And I don't feel like going to bed with you in the afternoon. I'm expecting some calls and ..."

Relationships tend to lose erotic intensity—for one partner or for both. Sustaining eroticism over the years takes effort. Sex is unpredictable; we may be sexually active during one period and totally inactive during another. In most marriages sexual activity ebbs and flows. Sex researcher John Money believes that romantic love—that heady, erotic absorption with another—lasts only about two years. Supposedly, nature has a built-in time limit for eroticism. During this period a strong bond is formed between a couple, and usually results in the birth of a child. After two years, the erotic attraction between the couple abates; increasingly, their relationship is based on friendship and security. If indeed a child has been born, the perpetuation of the species is ensured.

While we may have, according to Money, a primordial time clock, so do we have a modern consciousness. Since our society is not a primitive one wherein a husband, off on a hunt for dinner, becomes the quarry and never returns, we cannot think in terms of two-year time spans. Disallowing accidents or quirks of fate, most men will be around for quite a while. Therefore, we want the eroticism in our relationship to be ever-enveloping, ever-present—and it's just not.

Relationships become de-eroticized for a number of reasons other than the two-year theory. One reason has less to do with biology than with psychology—that is, women turn off because of their lowly positions at home. The woman who has no power in her relationship with her husband will seek control somewhere. Combine this search for power with her suppressed anger, and you can see how the bedroom becomes her stronghold. It follows that if her husband controls their money, their friendships, their decisions about the children, and the frequency of their sex life, the only things left for her to control are her body and her thoughts. In a marriage that lacks true intimacy, a woman may allow her husband to have sex with her, but she will never find it pleasurable, nor will she have an orgasm. Not caring that she is depriving herself of pleasure by thinking mundane, vengeful, or mindless thoughts to detach herself during sex, she is satisfied that she's denying her husband what he wants from her—her pleasure through his body.

Fear of intimacy may serve one partner as a means to desexualize the other. Though fears of closeness affect men more strongly, women too will sometimes flee from those moments of vulnerability. Usually there's a profound need to be held and stroked after orgasm—for men and for women. Those who fear intimacy may pull away immediately, get up, begin to chat as if no sexual experience had just been shared, or create some circumstance that will put distance between themselves and their partners. Liking or even loving the other person may have little to do with this behavior. There can be intense feelings, but they're routed or covered over. The greater the fear of intimacy and the greater the need to be with the partner, the more such a frightened soul may find a way to injure the relationship. The statement "I love you but I no longer desire you" is a bitter pill to swallow. Sex, then, is the final act of intimacy to go.

There are couples who insist they had wonderful sex lives with their partners until they married. Sex went downhill from there. Such couples, brought up in the belief that pre-marital sex is sinful or forbidden, find high excitement in flaunting the taboo, until they marry. Men caught in the "madonna/whore" complex may suffer the most. When a woman becomes, through marriage, a "good woman," i.e., a "madonna," her status becomes even more exalted when she bears children. At this point she is suddenly too "pure" for sex. In order to satisfy his sexual desires, the man will often go outside the marriage, seeking out "degraded" women. Usually what is occurring in such a man's mind is an unconscious identification of his wife with his mother, thus bringing into play the incest taboo, which prevents him from realizing sexual feelings toward his wife.

Women who have punitive, rigid, or critical husbands often lose sexual interest in them. Such women regard their husbands as authoritarian father figures, and cannot summon sexual feelings toward them.

In his book *Children of the Dream,* Bruno Bettelheim describes a fascinating phenomenon among people raised on an Israeli kibbutz. Even where there was childhood sexual play between males and females, no marriages occurred between any couple. Bettelheim's theory is that they subscribed to a voluntary incest taboo; this taboo prevented them as adults from considering each other as sexual partners. We may apply the same theory to ourselves. Because so many people marry when they're children, really, and grow up together, a fraternal bond is formed over the years, which breeds desexualization. The incest taboo again comes into play; one doesn't go to bed with one's brother or sister. However, if both partners are psychologically mature when they do create a marriage, there's less chance that this will happen.

WAITING TO WED

Here is the myth of the perfect marriage: First you are children together, then adults, then parents, then grandparents. At the turn of the century, when the average life span was about forty-seven years, it was only good sense to get married at seventeen, have children—a lot of them—almost immediately, and continue to live together until death. Today, when our average life span approaches seventy-seven years, it becomes increasingly a test of faith to live out one's marriage vows, which probably should now be rewritten to state "until *emotional* death do us part."

Or, as Sar A. Levitan and Richard S. Belous posit in their book *What's Happening to the American Family?:* "If marriage vows were dictated by the recorded facts [divorce rates], at least one-third of marrying couples would change the promise 'until death' to 'until we change partners.' Still, living as part of a family seems to be the preference of most adult Americans—and they like to play for keeps and to make it 'legal.' Despite a permissive society's toleration of experimentation, most individuals seem to prefer the traditional contractual relationship with all its obligations and restraints." Our problem is not in choosing the traditional family value system but in rushing into it at too early an age.

Our parents wanted to keep us children, ignorant of the ways of the world. At sixteen we were to have an engagement ring on our finger; by twenty-one we were to be married or we were considered old maids—or certainly trotting on the road to spinsterhood. So we were children when we married—uninformed and overprotected. We were first bounced on a parental knee, then tossed into the lap of another person from the same social background. As two young people with little sexual experience, we fumbled around, trying to find the secret to this "hot deal" called sex. Then, a year or so later, we became children who had our own children.

Marriage was to be a rite of passage to adulthood. It was to confer upon us wisdom, emotional strength, a new creation of family wherein the old mistakes by which our parents habitually lived would not be reenacted but diminished to nothing more than amusing anecdotes: "Remember how your mother had a fit if the dishes weren't washed instantly after dinner . . . when your father wanted an account of every penny he gave you?" Through marriage we escaped the parental bonds, physically at least, and attempted to experiment as well as we could. Suddenly, two decades passed between marriage at twenty years of age and discontent or confusion at forty. It was as if there were giant parentheses around those twenty years, before which was childhood and after which came old age. For many of us, those twenty years were a time when we did not know who we were.

"I'd met the man I was to marry when I was a senior in high school. I didn't know him, but that didn't matter," Debby, a midwestern woman, related. "I just wanted to get out of the house and add value to myself by getting a husband. Some of Lou's friend's were marrying young—nineteen- or twenty-year-olds who thought, Why not? So I decided to push. Lou wouldn't be the first in his group to get married, and I knew he wouldn't want to be the last. So we married. I was nineteen, Lou was one day over twenty-one.

"We made plans," she continued. "This marriage was going to be stable and secure for both of us. I agreed to work until Lou could move up in his job. Sex was a disaster for me that first year; I didn't know what was going on and I was afraid to ask questions. One thing was wonderful, though. Lou was civilized, basically willing to talk things out, and there was no screaming or irrational shouting. I'd come from that kind of environment and was glad for the peace of Lou's company."

Debby's story soon became similar to those of many other women. She asked her husband for permission to do things: "Is it okay if I visit with Roz?" (Or "take a drive?" or "buy a dress?") Lou's goals were her goals; she related to him as a father-protector. As with many bright, self-scrutinizing woman, Debby didn't understand her growing discontent with her life until she was thirty-nine years old—after twenty years of married life. "Luckily I chose well. Lou became successful in his business and was a pretty good husband," she told me. "The more he rose in the world, the faster I tried to make myself into the kind of woman he'd want me to be. Sometimes I fell short of his ideal. I wasn't sophisticated enough in some situations, or knowledgeable enough in others. I only wanted to be the woman who'd make him comfortable and do whatever it took to get him there. I didn't want to speak or behave in a way that would embarrass him. It wasn't until we were married about fifteen years that I realized how lonely I was. It wasn't Lou's fault. I'd pushed for marriage. There was no sacrifice I could make that was too great—but I became bitter. I cried every day, felt angry and deprived—exactly the way I felt when I was a child. I married young because it was the thing to do. Half of my reason was to leave my parents' home, but I rushed into another kind of prison. I was totally unprepared for the reality of living through another person."

Thus, many of us had a childhood and a quasi-adulthood within marriage. Never did we have the opportunity to experiment with sex, career pursuits, traveling, even religion. Nonexperimentation is fine as long as society stays the same, but if it changes, for one to want a taste of those changes is predictable. Women have started to express their quandaries: "I don't know who I am other than someone's daughter, someone's wife, and someone's mother. Where's that place in life that's going to be mine?" That place, for many women, doesn't appear until they're forty-seven or fifty years old. The problem now is not having a "place" but what to do within it.

Typically, we've lived sequentially: childhood, marriage, parenthood, children leaving the nest, then self-exploration through schooling or a job. Another more open approach to life might make more sense: childhood, self-exploration, discriminating sexual experience, marriage, further self-exploration, parenthood, greater emotional growth, children leaving the nest, further goal-setting.

"Keep your twenties to yourself," a friend of mine's father once advised her about not getting married until she was at least thirty years old, with some idea of what life was all about. "I thought this was a radical philosophy, coming from a man who'd married at twenty-two to a woman a year older—my mother. I grew up in the 1950s when women not only married young but looked down their noses at those of us who opted for our own apartments and jobs. I took my father's advice, knowing that if I desperately wanted to get married, I could. There was always someone to marry, if marriage was my main goal. I put it off until I was thirty-eight, and it was both a blessing and a serious shock to my system. Mostly, I knew who I was and what I wanted from a man, but on the other hand, it was I who had to stop living on my schedule and make some adjustments for another person's needs."

In *Ms.* magazine there appeared a revealing article consisting of a series of interviews with women who were over thirty-five when they married for the first time. It was called, "Why I Got Married Now." Marlo Thomas, a connubial late-bloomer, wrote of her marriage to Phil Donahue: "First I had to see that marriage wasn't something that *happened* to you—but something two people could *design* for themselves. Second, the world had to change—so that the old patterns for marriage relaxed and men and women didn't feel guilty if they broke them. Then I had to meet a man who had followed a different path to arrive at the same conclusion. . . ." And of her choice of men, Esther Margolis, president of her own publishing company, Newmarket Publishing and Communications, said: "I think two years before I would have passed [Stan] by because he wasn't like other men I had gone out with. I had been ducking men like Stan. I wasn't aware of how strong they were. I might have presumed that because they were so supportive of their women, that that was a sign of weakness." Married at forty-two years old, Ms. Margolis described the man she married as someone she originally thought was "too nice."

If we know who we are, it is likely that the men we choose will be similarly secure in their own identities. By the time we are thirty, it is reasonable for a man to expect that we can handle finances. By this time, also, we will have had a number of sexual encounters; a man will realize this, and will also realize that it is our choice to share a bed with him now. Sex will thus be given its rightful place as part of a relationship, and not the sole reason to marry. If our man loves to eat sushi and we find raw fish appalling, we needn't worry about being talked into taking a bite to be a "good sport"; we can merely go along with him while he indulges his taste. Essentially, a man will respect our preferences, and we his, no matter how divergent they may be. But if you marry young and adapt yourself to a man, you may soon find that you have little of yourself left to call your own.

We like to think of the family as a loving, peaceful sanctuary wherein each member can be free of life's stresses; in fact, it can also be a center of violence. There are two reasons: The first is inequality and the second is an image of maleness in America, which sanctions physical abuse. Studies show that violence is more likely to occur in homes in which one person holds the power and makes all the decisions. Democratic households, however, in which decision-making is shared, reveal significantly less violence.

So, if you marry as equals, you can expect less violence. But if you marry on a parent-child level—the husband in the parental role and the wife in the child's position—and make an attempt at independence before your spouse is ready to accept it, there will be a greater chance of brutality. Violence is the only way for many men to say, "I've made a big investment in this relationship, and I'm afraid to lose you to another man or to a job or to some other circumstance that tempts you." When a woman disturbs the neurotic fiber of a relationship, her husband may become afraid of losing his power. Few people lose power gracefully.

Marriages between two adults are far more likely to succeed because there is less of a power struggle, less of a need to resolve issues through violence. Marriages between adults allow for continual change within the relationship. By giving yourself a chance for exploration before marriage, you enter this union knowing more about who you are and what you need from a partner. By knowing who you are and how to take care of yourself financially, you put less stress on yourself and on your spouse; you can contribute. By waiting to wed until you know you're the main course, your opportunity for sexual and emotional fulfillment is greater. By waiting to wed, you become *ready* to wed.

Chapter Eight

If He Calls You a Bitch, Say "Thank You!"

Once upon a time, men used to foster the notion that women were a species of jungle cat, eager to claw each other to ribbons on those rare occasions, such as bridge parties, when they were allowed out without their trainers. The strategy was simple: divide and conquer. Keep the gals busy trying to scratch each others' eyes out, and they'll never notice who put the bars on the cage.
—Anne Beatts, from "Women, Friendship, and Bitchiness," an article in Vogue

What alarms men is the possibility that women may be more clearsighted. [Men] can be fairly sure of respect from their male colleagues in the hierarchy, who hardly even see them as human beings, after all, and can therefore accept or ignore their physical and emotional peculiarities. But might not a woman see them somewhat more plainly?
—Michael Korda, Power! How to Get It, How to Use It

Women in the job market or those thinking of switching careers may have good intentions, but unless there is a clearly defined goal, there's trouble ahead. Among these women are the fatalists—those who take what's offered because they've run into it head-on. It may be the wrong job for them, but it's a sure thing. Then there are women with grandiose dreams, who hear only the applause to come and don't know how to organize for success. Here is a vivid example of how *not* to begin a new career:

Sarah had an idea about opening a health-food bar in a busy shopping mall. Her scheme included counter seating, no waiters or waitresses, and no chef (therefore, no kitchen), but easy-to-prepare salads, drinks, and yogurt sundaes. All dishes would be tossed together by a few food-preparers who'd man the counters. Sarah, a social worker, did not want to give up her job until she knew the salad bar was a success. If it took off, she could either manage it full-time or invest some of the profits in yet another similarly run operation. Meanwhile, deciding she needed a partner, Sarah spoke with Louise, a woman professionally connected to a diet center. Louise was enthusiastic about the idea, but offered a few suggestions to "improve" the concept:

The mall location was out. Why not open at a large tennis club? If it was to be at a tennis club, then it would follow, Louise said, presenting her logic, that the clientele would not like sitting at counters; give them tables. Of course, this would mean hiring waitresses. But now that they're seated at tables, the men, especially, would not be satisfied with just salads and yogurt, but would want a substantial meal. So far, Sarah's modest "success formula" for a fast-food health bar had escalated into an elaborate plan for an expensive restaurant. Louise suggested they bring in a third partner for practicality. Sarah had intended to partially finance the place and bring in a manager—her job precluded her being there full-time. Louise, employed at a diet center, could not be there to oversee operations either. They needed a working partner, so they asked Joanna to join them.

Joanna had visions of being the next Julia Child, but with a Hungarian touch. Her specialties were goulash and cream pastries; her only philosophy about food was to serve it in large portions. Since Joanna would be responsible for the cooking and the management, Sarah and Louise needed assurance that she could handle money. Joanna, though not a bookkeeper, insisted she could keep track of all the accounts in her head. Joanna's financial system was random and improvised, but Sarah and Louise nevertheless agreed to it. They found a tennis club and made a deal with the owner to put in the restaurant. Next, to guarantee that the owner of the club wouldn't raise the rent on them, Sarah, Louise, and Joanna invited the owner's wife, Liz, to become the fourth partner. By this time Sarah had come a long way from carrot cake and yogurt frappés.

Each of the four women invested $6,000; of the total $24,000, $20,000 went for equipment alone. The restaurant opened at the end of August. By the end of October, Liz announced she was getting ready to go off on her yearly four-month trip to Florida. Said Liz, "Business isn't going to stop me from going away. I winter in Florida, and this year will be no different." At about this time, the three other partners were worrying about the profits—there weren't any. The place was popular and had a limited but fairly good menu, so money should have been rolling in. Joanna, the chef and manager, was the most befuddled. Her money-managing system usually worked, although she was hard-pressed ever to find the bills from the food suppliers, among others. Louise, still at the diet center, was the angriest. Her approach was to scold Joanna, to call her a fool, then to storm out of the restaurant. Sarah, the most in control, tried to help Joanna with the paperwork—that is, when Joanna could find the proper papers.

In a way, the original quartet represented what's right and what's wrong with women dabbling in business. Among them they had invested $24,000, and eight months later they owed $48,000. In less than a year they'd lost $72,000, a debt due mostly to bad management, individual competition, and egocentric aims. Each had a different vision, and the restaurant failed because there was no teamwork.

In November, Joanna crumbled from the pressure, a nervous wreck. By December, the restaurant was two partners short; the other two were frantically searching for someone to run the business. By the following April, they were $48,000 in debt.

Sarah commented: "Now that I look back, I see that we weren't responsible for each other, though we all had a single goal—to open a restaurant. None of us knew how to make that goal work, nor did we know at what point we should have given up and closed the door with dignity. Our worst mistake was jumping into a business about which we knew nothing and had not one shred of experience."

About inexperience, Carole Hyatt states in her book *Women & Work:* "People crash when they fly blind. You have to be willing to take the time to put in an apprenticeship, so you will know what you are doing when you fly solo. . . . The best ideas in the world turn into nightmares when people fail to do their homework, to make sure they can make a living from what they do. They let enthusiasm override good sense. . . . People fail when they don't research their motivations as well as their market." And of partners she says: "In many respects, a working business partner is the same as a marriage partner. You must be able to live very closely together on a daily basis. . . . Although your partner's irritating personal habits are literally not your business, you have to keep them from affecting your relationship, just as you would in a marriage."

One truism that applies to Sarah's venture into business and to many others like it is that *women do not support women.* This lack of mutual support, as much as inexperience, served to doom their business. Two decades or so ago, many women would rather have had their heads shaved than function as a supportive member of an all-female team. Though women's feelings toward one another have ostensibly changed from distrust and competitiveness to compassion and helpfulness, Sarah and her partners lapsed into the old clichés about women working together. The restaurant was no longer a business, but the scene of a shark fight. Everyone bled.

Competitiveness, even among women who work together as equals, is a problem. Even fiercer competition is apparent between women who have achieved and those still fighting toward their goals. Successful women often do not wish to graciously mold the talents of other women on the way up. And those on the way up may not play fair toward those already at the top.

Sandy has an executive position with an advertising agency. Over the last year, she's had a number of offers from other companies, and has at times considered going elsewhere. If someone in a position of power indicates, overtly or covertly, that better opportunities await her, her present employer will often negotiate with her. The company will be frank and say something like "We hear you've been shaking the bushes. We'd like to have you stay with us, so let's discuss what you don't like and what you want." In Sandy's case, no such meeting occurred. The company hired a junior person to be groomed for her position. "They are," Sandy said succinctly, "trying to head me off at the pass."

Sandy did not know at first that Iris had been hired to be her replacement; she learned of it through office scuttlebutt. "Naturally," Sandy said, "I went to my boss and asked him why he was edging me out. He denied it. I've been in the business long enough to know what's going on. I see how they're training her. Most of all, and most obvious, Iris does not speak to me at all. She ignores me except when she needs something pertaining to a client. Why would she do this, unless she's part of the company conspiracy and she's embarrassed to face me, knowing she's about to move into my office when I leave? I believe she's fallen for the company line about her being promoted to my job when my contract is up—within a year—and is smug as hell about it."

Sandy's thinking differs from that of the company. "My boss has asked me to give a critique of Iris's work to help *me,* they say. I won't do it. They're suggesting that I should be a good team player by letting Iris hit all the home runs. By improving Iris's work, of course, I'd be cutting my own throat. Though it's unspoken, the company is saying to me, 'Are you not a participating member of the team? And if you are, why won't you step aside to let Iris move up? New talent makes the company grow. Don't you want to see the company grow?' Sure I do, but not without me, and not with Iris in my shoes.

"Interestingly enough," Sandy went on, "the company played the old game of pitting women against women—a lethal mistake. Perhaps they think I'm getting too big for my britches and they intend to show me how little clout I really have by grooming someone for my job. Because they hired Iris the way they did, I feel no need to participate in the formation and development of her abilities. When people ask me what I think of Iris, I always say I think she's terrific. But I wouldn't lift a finger to correct her mistakes."

Iris's biggest blunder was her assumption that Sandy was on her way out and therefore not worth cultivating as a friend or mentor. Instead of having an ally, Iris may wind up caught in the middle. "If she were a fine strategist," Sandy added wisely, "she would play both ends. She could play ball with the company and with me. Had she made an attempt to meet me, know me, she'd have found out that I don't begrudge her advance in the company—if it happens. Under other circumstances, I'd have happily been her mentor. As a senior staffer, I could have clued her in to company tactics. She could have tested them out within a safety zone as a junior member. I could have taught her what she needs to know. As it is, she's dazzled by the company's promises to her, but I promise *you,* they will screw her to the wall."

Iris made a typical female error. As men prove themselves to other men, so do women prove themselves to men. If she believed in herself, she'd not have adopted the male style of advancing through the ranks, and she'd have found herself an ally. Instead, Iris fell for the company line the way a naïve nineteen-year-old believes a man will care for her forever when they marry.

Mary Cunningham, a vice-president at Joseph E. Seagram and Sons, said in an address to the Commonwealth Club of San Francisco that "joining an organization is like being born into a family or taking on citizenship. With that joining, you take on new responsibilities, the most serious of which is to work for the good of the organization. This does not absolve you from adherence to principle. Nor does it deny your individual rights. It just amends them. . . . I am convinced that as [a] notion of common purpose takes hold, we will find that we are building a new kind of cooperation. The organization will become more humane, more like a family—and this is [one] condition I believe is required in order to reverse the trend toward indifference and create, instead, a climate for increased productivity.

"The analogy to the family is a risky one for a woman to make—it evokes sentimental, non-businesslike stereotypes. But families have functioned as economic units throughout the history of our species. And because the members had to pull together to survive, cooperation became a necessity— and skills were not wasted."

Had Iris been clever and more humane, she wouldn't have allowed herself to be trapped by a possible corporate bluff, but would have known that her own best interests might not be served by her taking over Sandy's spot. Had she seen herself as part of a family, Iris might have found in Sandy a valuable ally and advisor. As things stood, however, Sandy's skills might well be lost to the company because they would not be passed down, as a family legacy is. And if Sandy did stay, with the company's blessings, Iris could be out on the street. "What if I stipulate that the only condition under which I'll stay is that Iris goes?" Sandy speculated. "They may not like firing her, but they may want to lose me less than they want to lose her. I don't know if I'm capable of getting Iris fired, but it's obviously crossed my mind. I used to feel," she concluded, "that a person really learned lessons about the world out of kindness, but I no longer know if that's true."

Sandy's boss, and possibly Iris, undoubtedly think of Sandy as a bitch for not cooperating and capitulating. Were Sandy not a bitch by their definition—firm in her position, selfishly motivated, betraying the company's interests by not assisting Iris—she'd be eager to be a "good sport" about Iris's presence. How would Sandy feel about the appellation? "Annoyed," she said. "I think of my position more in terms of self-preservation. But so be it."

I would like to offer another perspective on the word *bitch*. The next time a man at the office spits out "Bitch!" or mumbles it under his breath just loud enough for you to doubt whether you've heard it at all, congratulate yourself, if he's referring to you. You've received a compliment. It probably means you've demonstrated competence, effectiveness, and assertiveness. The man is therefore feeling inadequate or cornered. Since he's not prepared to deal with a woman who knows what she's talking about, especially if she proves him wrong, he's agitated and threatened. If he's threatened, his power is on the line, and when that line is drawn by a woman, she is, in his eyes, a bitch. As Michael Korda says in *Power! How to Get It, How to Use It,*

"Pushed hard enough, [men] will give way on money, titles, large offices, expense accounts—anything but power. So long as a man can have the final word, he is reasonably content to give up anything else, though not of course without a struggle."

The woman who is deliberately cutting, emasculating, belittling, and vicious on her way to the top, the woman who is guilty of premeditated sabotage of another woman's career, who spreads gossip, who establishes exclusivity among a few co-workers to keep close competitors out is, indeed, a bitch. This is not the sort of woman I'm referring to. Such women must search their own consciences in their striving for power—and see what it costs them and others around them. Rather, I refer to the woman who knows her job, has a reasonable grasp of what power is and how to use it, and is rational, effective, and schooled in the logistics of business.

A man is admired for displaying good business sense. Men have long equated greatness in industry with the ability to "drive a hard bargain," "rule with an iron fist," "keep an ear to the ground," "be a tough negotiator," and "tell it like it is." What of women who possess such skills? Men still hold to the notion that assertiveness and the ability to use logic are biologically determined traits—male traits. The woman who dares to defy this notion is therefore a "bitch"; "she thinks she knows it all." In fact, in a man's eyes, she may know too much, or she may know just enough to get his job. A man who has the power to provoke feelings of inadequacy in another man is one thing; a woman who has the power to arouse such feelings in a man is the worst kind of creature . . . a bitch.

A man may feel frustrated when a woman shows that she

is as proficient as he in an area he considers his own territory. Not surprisingly, he will respond with anger. However, women have an obligation to themselves to demonstrate their capabilities to the fullest. It is not prudent to try to outdo men for the sport of it, but a woman should be true to herself and secure in her abilities. And if a man feels that his toes are being stepped on, that's business.

The point is not to turn demonstrable competence into damning competition. Baiting a man just to show him up is playing dirty.

Ideally, the qualities that draw admiring glances in the business world should be redefined to include both men and women. The truth is that a woman can be competitive and feminine too. No one remarks disparagingly about the male executive who "shoots from the hip" during the day and becomes tender and affectionate with his family at home; somehow, casual observers don't see an inconsistency here. But if a woman displays the same behavior, she must be sexually frustrated, unnatural, fulfilling her wish to be a man, relentlessly trying to prove something—a bitch. But an unbiased appraisal reveals that she's fulfilling herself by working intelligently and productively. And if she's called a bitch for that, her only answer should be "Thank you."

OUT OF THE NEST

There are three critical adjustments a woman must make when she ceases to be full-time housewife and moves out into the business world: focusing her energies in a definite direction, coping with the emotional difficulties inherent in the prospect of working, and understanding the difference between a job and a career. In examining these difficult but necessary adjustments, we will begin with the last, which is also the easiest: job versus career.

If you toil away at a desk, counting the minutes till Friday rolls around, and you spot the payroll clerk ambling toward you with your check in hand, you've got a job. If you have little interest in the company's business, other than hoping it remains profitable so you can smile on Fridays, you've got a job. If you have no aspirations to go beyond where you are, but merely seek affirmation and appreciation, you've still got a job.

When you take on a career, you awaken each day eager to progress and excel at what you do. A career is as much a part of your identity as the sound of your voice or the way you wear your hair. Though a career is something you desire to have, enjoy working at, and love to learn more about, it entails a certain commitment of time and energy. A career means extended hours and cancelled appointments with friends. It also means, at moments, that you are getting paid for work you'd gladly do without pay. A career has more than one home—it does not get locked up in a desk drawer at five o'clock to be tidied up the next day. A career travels with you, on the train home, at home, during lunch—even, on occasion, over weekends.

Finding a sense of direction—that is, discovering what you really want to do—is more problematic. Many women improvise, taking a series of jobs until one strikes their fancy. Often this is the path of least resistance—perhaps an insurance company has an opening and you pass their test for eligibility, but you have no interest in insurance. Some women enroll in courses with titles like "Investigations into Myself." Such courses are often valuable for the undirected woman. Within these courses are aptitude tests that are worth the tuition. Testing reveals interests and abilities and how they may fit together for profitable use. From there, the next step is to speak with a counselor who understands how you should proceed. These questions may be asked: What, realistically, can you accomplish at your age? What is your situation at home—the finances, the responsibilities toward children and husband, the mutual goals between you and your spouse? When you've made your decision, can it be acted on immediately or does it require long-term planning?

One woman in her late thirties told me she'd decided to attend law school—but she'd never worked from the day she married, at age twenty-two. She told me: "I wasn't sure how to tell the news to my family. Should I prepare them for it right then and set up a system that would help us function better when I started school six months later or just drop the news on them a few weeks before the term began? One thing was certain—I needed my husband's financial aid. I'd inherited some money from my father, but just enough to get me through one year of school. I decided to tell them what I intended to do, rather than wait. At first my husband was amused by my ambitions; he said, 'You can't talk your way out of a speeding ticket. How the hell will you get a client off?' I controlled myself and answered, 'Maybe you're right. If I fail, I'll end up being wrong and I won't mention it again. It won't cost you a penny. If I don't fail, will you help me through the next two years?' He said it was okay with him. I'm about to finish my second year of school, and so far the kids and my husband are being cooperative."

Since women have often thought of work as a punishment rather than as a reward, as a disgrace rather than as something honorable—as having sold their very lives for bitter wages rather than having exchanged their skills for a commensurate salary—approaching work at all is full of emotional jolts. Virginia Valian, a psychologist, put it well in her commentary that appeared in *Working it Out,* edited by Sara Ruddick and Pamela Daniels. She tells of her history as a working woman, of her battle to accomplish something, and of how she eventually solved the problems. She says: "I approached work usually with two sorts of feelings. One was anger and resentment that I had to work; the other was a sense of competition as a life-or-death struggle—either I would kill others or they would kill me. Winning meant betraying the lives of those who were failures in the eyes of the world; it also meant that others would be jealous and envious of me, would want to destroy me. Losing meant that I was pathetic and unworthy. For most of my life my way of coping with that picture was neither to win nor to lose completely, to be smart and clever but to accomplish nothing. In other words, I could not renounce the picture, but I could embody the contradiction it evoked."

As you get past the contradictions, resentments, and fears, you begin to see work as an enriching aspect of life. It's the sense of a job well done, the knowledge that you've had a productive day that's inched you forward and contributed to a sense of growth and development. You are *more* as a result.

Where do you fit in when you are ready for the business world? Two basic types of personalities prevail in business—the entrepreneur and the manager. The entrepreneur often has difficulties functioning within a corporation since she sees it as a benevolent police state. The corporation, characterized by ascending echelons of authority, dictates to its employees how they must act to survive within it; employees will be told when to arrive and leave, when to take lunch, how fast they may or may not rise, exactly what they must do. The entrepreneurial type, finding this rigid structure limiting and cumbersome, may do well within that structure, but not without feeling distressed, even trapped. The managerial personality is happy to comply with company policy: this person, the security, continuity, and familiarity are worth adherence to the rules. While the entrepreneur will take risks for her own benefit, the manager can only take those risks if they will also benefit the company—that is, if she wants to stay there.

Before leaving the nest, many women have no idea where they fit in best or whether they must construct a professional life on their own—should they join a company or open their own. Others, committed to success, strike out against all odds and win. Such a woman is Heidi Stein, a remarkable study in the rewards of following one's own star.

Lebanese by birth, Heidi was brought to this country when she was fifteen years old, the child bride in a marriage arranged for her by her parents. "In the culture I was brought up in, it was only okay to get an education to prepare yourself to marry, not to work," she said. "I grew up in a house with three brothers who could do what they wanted. I wanted to do what I wanted, too. When I came to America, things didn't change much for me. My husband wanted an old-country wife, but I was more interested in freeing myself for a a career. Hope and ambition kept me alive. Being successful was important to me. I took a course in hairdressing, and that, basically, changed my life. I'd found my career.

"When I was nineteen, I decided to open my own beauty shop. I'd been working for another shop and I'd saved my money, but didn't have enough to go into business. My husband, still hot for old-country ways, didn't approve at all. He wouldn't sign for a loan for me, but that didn't stop me. I'd befriended the man who ran the gas station near my house and I asked him to sign for me. He did. I opened my shop, and six months later it was burned down in the Detroit riots.

"I needed another shop and another loan. I went to the bank, this time on my own, and asked for the money. The loan officer turned me down. I demanded to speak to the president of the bank. I showed him that I could run a business and pay my debts, which I still had on the first loan. I got my money. In three months I was out of debt, and pretty soon I opened another shop. Now I have seven shops in Michigan and seven more across the country."

Heidi characterizes herself as someone committed to a goal, a woman who, because of temperament and talent, must be in a position where she makes the rules and does not follow those devised by others. She is also resourceful and unflappable, qualities that make her the epitome of the entrepreneurial spirit.

While Heidi was fired by ambition, Zena, a West Coast woman, was motivated by money. Born into a working-class family where it was not uncommon for the utilities to be turned off for nonpayment, Zena married at seventeen years of age to a man she thought would give her security. By a twist of fate, her husband wound up in a low-paying job. Now, with two children to care for, Zena, at the age of twenty-one, knew she'd have to get a job to make ends meet.

"I didn't want to work, but I swore I'd never be poor again. I'd only graduated from high school and had never worked. I wasn't equipped to do much, so I took a good look at myself and realized that what I did have was a good face. I started to model. I wasn't making a fortune since I'm not the high-fashion type, but it was something. I searched for another job that would pay more and be more interesting than modeling. I went to radio-announcing school, got a job in radio, then moved into TV. By a fluke, the producer of a show quit and I was asked to take it over. I was making money and actually loving work now.

"After a few years in TV," Zena continued, "I met a man, an executive at an advertising agency. I began working with him, placing commercials on TV while still at my producing job. Within six years I'd gone from earning about a hundred dollars a week to making a few million a year in commissions. Eventually I left TV and joined him to form our own agency.

"What's amazing to me is that I'd never planned my career at all. Situations made themselves available to me and I took every chance there was to advance. I see each new situation as a challenge. I like to work, to solve problems—and have it come out profitable."

I asked her how she felt about power. She replied: "If anything, I don't feel powerful, although I know I have a position of power. The truth about power for me is that it allows me to make my own decisions while my earning capacity gives me access to structure my life my way. While people in the business call me 'the velvet hammer' because I'm very soft-spoken but tough and honest, I don't feel that awesome sense of power. Maybe if I did, I'd stop striving and coast along. One thing I know—underneath all my success is that old fear of not having. That keeps me moving forward."

Not every woman who seeks a career, or who seeks a job and fortuitously finds a career, has intentions of climbing to the top slot. To such women, middle-level positions are satisfying, ego-gratifying, and remunerative enough. To such women, the title on the door isn't worth being away from home or giving up solitary pursuits. Others, starting from ground level, are still working through problems with their husbands about working at all. Ruth is such a case.

"A year ago, the thought of a job would make me shudder. But now that I have a job, marriage is driving me wild!" Ruth laughed lightly, as if to deflate the seriousness of her predicament, a predicament many women share, then continued: "First my husband said to me in an urgent tone, 'The economy is bad and my business isn't going well. If you want to continue living as we are, you'll have to help out.' I resisted, I'm not quite sure why, except that I'd only worked for a year before we married and I couldn't think of a thing I could do or would want to do. I got so used to staying at home with my son, who's six now, and structuring my life around him, around lunches and dinners with friends, and around a little shopping and tennis, that the idea of going out *there* was threatening. So finally I thought, time to grow up and take care of myself and stop living off Tim.

"I scrounged around for something to do. After all, no one was about to hire me as a vice-president at General Motors. I found this little job, working in a dress shop at one of the local malls. It was perfect. They only needed me three days a week, and luckily my hours were flexible enough so I could come in after my son left for school and leave in time to be home when school let out. Okay, it paid minimum wage, but so what? It was my second attempt at working, and to tell the truth, I didn't do badly at all."

Within three months on her job, Ruth was asked to design window displays and do some modeling. She really began to like the job and the variety of responsibilities the owners delegated to her.

"So here I was," she said, "suddenly playing the supermom. I was working part-time, pulling in a little money, putting some of it toward bills, and banking some of it for myself. I was caring for the house, although things weren't quite as organized, quite as spotless, and quite as on-time as they had been in the past. At first, Tim was knocked out. His little 'nincompoop,' as he so fondly called me, was actually out there working.

"Just when I thought everything was falling into place, Tim pulled some old macho tricks. I was working and he liked the money part—but I was working, liking it, and getting somewhere, which he didn't. Suddenly, he began to make demands on me. This was the man who was once too rushed to have breakfast at home, now asking me to make breakfast for him when I was about to race out of the house to get to work. Suddenly I was 'no fun' anymore. Suddenly I was a 'lousy sexual partner.'

"Now it's a full-time wife that he wants, not an equal partner. In a moment of frustration and desperation, I asked him if he wanted a divorce. He said, 'If you want one, do it now and don't wait. I'd just as soon get it over with and not wonder when you're going to drop the news on me.' "

Ruth's husband, Tim, was a practical man ("We need what money you can bring in"), who transformed his negative emotional reaction to his wife's independence into an accusation of negligence on her part ("Why aren't you here when I need you? Who cares about the money?"). Tim was threatened, Ruth was confused. Tim felt deprived, Ruth felt sabotaged. Tim would have liked Ruth's salary to materialize without Ruth's having to go out and earn it; Ruth wanted to work, but wished Tim would stop "driving her crazy." Lack of communication, it would appear, was endangering their marriage. It was up to Ruth, then, to clarify their goals and individual needs without either of them feeling a loss. Though both might suffer from Ruth's lack of income until Tim was in a stronger financial position, it was Ruth who would lose her self-esteem if she should forfeit her job to "save" the marriage. Again, she would be Tim's "nincompoop"—a woman incapable of doing anything right.

Ruth's approach, like that of many women in similar straits, was to take the offensive. By accusing Tim of creating disorder in her life, or threatening divorce—a threat she was barely prepared to carry out—she further irritated Tim, who felt offended enough by Ruth's "abandoning" him to a job. Ruth had proved that she could contribute to the household financially, while Tim awaited proof that he was still needed.

If economic independence was an equalizer, how could Tim accept Ruth as a nonthreatening partner, and not as a usurper of masculine power? Such men as Tim must be spoken to in language they understand.

Here is Ruth's case for her continuing on the job: (1) It's important for her to be perceived by Tim as a capable woman, not as an incompetent. (2) Should something unfortunate happen to Tim, he will suffer less, knowing that Ruth can carry some of the load. (3) Should something happen to Ruth, Tim will go on as before, though inconvenienced for a short time—in Ruth's eyes, she is far more replaceable in her role as mother, wife, and housekeeper than Tim is as a father, husband, and provider. (4) Instead of edging into the job market when she is in her forties, fifties, or sixties, when there may be even less opportunity for women with no work experience, she has a chance now to develop her skills at little sacrifice to her family's well-being. (5) She wants Tim to be pleased that he has an equal partner in this marriage, not another dependent.

Lack of prudent communication also afflicts the woman who does not know how to sell herself properly for a job. Though her husband has no argument against her reaching for as great a goal as she can grasp, Norma, in her eagerness to get ahead, engineered her own defeat.

At the age of forty, Norma, who'd been working part-time for the previous fifteen years of her marriage, decided to do some volunteer work for a local radio station. Impressed with her organizational ability and enthusiasm, the station asked her to sit in for a producer who was ill. Norma learned fast; within a few months, she was a full-time staffer when another producer left.

Then Norma heard about a job at a local TV station. Though she had no experience with television production, Norma thought she'd give the job a try. The position available was that of audience coordinator for live shows. She managed to get an interview, but not the job. I asked her what she'd said.

Norma told me that since her real interests were in production, and not in audience coordination, she saw nothing inappropriate about mentioning it to the interviewer. How had she mentioned it? "I told them that if they hired me for the coordinator's job, I'd work for them, on my own time, for no money, to learn how to produce a TV show," she said. She was convinced this was an ingenious strategy. She was wrong.

A company may be interested in your aspirations, but they do not want to hear that you're using the job that's open as a foot in the door. This, basically, is what Norma was relating by offering her services, though on her own time, gratis. The station was not looking to make a deal—hiring Norma and paying her a salary while sharing her excitement about her training herself for a power position at no cost to them. Any astute interviewer would have to speculate about Norma's possible performance as an audience coordinator. Would she do a sloppy job, for which she was being paid, so she could dash off to observe a production in progress? Norma wagered that the station would be charmed by her enthusiasm, and she lost.

Had she been smarter, Norma would have sold the very skill that got her hired in radio—she could *coordinate,* and do it efficiently. The goal, at that interview, was to get the job, not bargain for a better one. Within six months of working in TV, Norma would have had a sense of how every aspect of the station worked. By then, perhaps, she'd have befriended a producer who might have offered her an apprenticeship on her own time. Jane Adams, in her book *Women on Top,* gives us this insight into goal-setting: "Successful women depict their careers in terms of goals they have accomplished rather than fantasies they have fulfilled." Norma's thinking was the reverse: She pictured her career in terms of a fantasy to be fulfilled, and disregarded her considerable accomplishments in radio.

A FEW WORDS ON FAILING

"I would rather fail than not be among the greatest," the poet John Keats wrote in a letter. The sentiment, for many, is as applicable to them as it was to Keats, who, as it turned out, *was* among the greatest. Keats thought in the extreme—either be great or be nothing. He was lucky.

Failing is unpleasant. The prospect of failure is so unpleasant to some women that they would rather not attempt a task (a relationship, a diet), but would prefer to stay where or as they are rather than face possible defeat. Failing, they label themselves failures. Here, they say, is the incriminating evidence to prove my point: I failed, therefore I am a failure.

Success stories almost always include tales of failure: a lost job, a missed opportunity, a financial setback, wrong timing, mismanagement, being overlooked for promotion, somehow never quite being eligible for the job that was sought after. Failure stories from those who fear failure rarely include tales of success: learning from the experience, coming to know one's own limitations and abilities, applying what was learned to achieve the next time, developing an instinct about when to reach forward and when to mark time.

Success stories inspire both admiration and envy. True tales of success that qualify as inspirational usually involve the mentally or physically handicapped who triumph over their disabilities in some remarkable way. Virginia Valian, in *Working It Out,* commented that sometimes she had a fantasy about being physically handicapped and successful. "After all," she wrote, "who could feel jealous of me if I became paralyzed from the neck down?" In one way, the "overwhelming-odds syndrome," of which she speaks in her fantasy, allowed her to finish a specific amount of work, which, for her at the time, indicated a measure of success.

Success stories—those that do not highlight people less fortunate than ourselves—tend to inspire envy. And that's fine. The problem is in viewing ourselves as failures in comparison to those who succeed. Many women who fear failure find themselves immobilized psychologically. For that reason, they don't make an effort. By making no attempt at success, many think themselves safe from either success or failure—they straddle the fence, cautiously inching along, being neither too salient a success nor too conspicuous a washout. By staying where they are, they needn't test the range of their skills, needn't confront an abiding fear that they won't measure up to another's standards. Of course, by not going beyond where they happen to be, they will never discover whether they can become not a failure but a success.

At the core of this fear of failure is a sense that one is not worthy of success: "When they find out I really can't do this, I'm done for." "How did I get that award? Is the committee mad?" "I only got this promotion by a fluke." The old negative messages about who we are and what we can do resonate yet again. And intense feelings of insecurity, whether or not they are covered by a veneer of confidence or bravado, influence our relationship to success. Some theorists suggest that the fear of failure and the fear of success are interchangeable. Success entails responsibilities, pressures, challenges, split-second decisions. If these conditions of success are not met, the consequence is failure. Successful people invariably have in themselves some driving force that motivates them in their quest for success—recognition, riches, a need for excellence, a love of fulfilling work, even revenge. When the drive is great enough, a temporary defeat does not mean the war is over. They will re-arm for the next battle. Those convinced that they are failures will be unable to negotiate success, should it occur, and unconsciously trip themselves up: "I was never good at deadlines." "I'd have gotten to the top except for my inability to get anywhere on time." "No one ever tells me how to do things. I can't be expected to find out for myself." "I'm not taking on extra work on the off chance that I'll get a raise and promotion. They're just out to exploit me."

I've learned one lesson in life: If you want a place in the sun, you must be prepared to get a few blisters. When you want to achieve in your way, you'll know that minor burns heal fast.

The greatest difficulty confronting women lies in opting for autonomy, and it's a prerequisite for success. Independence implies that others can no longer dictate who you are—you *know* who you are. This takes courage. As Susan B. Anthony said: "Cautious, careful people always casting about to preserve their reputation can never bring about reform. Those in earnest are willing to be anything or nothing, publicly or privately, and avow their sympathy to deeper ideas and bear the consequences."

To make things happen and to reform your life, always takes courage. But when you have faith in yourself, and you can develop it, no "cautious, careful people" can stop you. It's within your power to be more, and no one knows that better than you!

Chapter Nine

Staying Sane in an Insane World

In brief, people with self-respect exhibit a certain tough-
ness, a kind of moral nerve; they display what was once
called character, *a quality which, although approved in the ab-*
stract, sometimes loses ground to other, more instantly ne-
gotiable virtues. The measure of its slipping prestige is that
one tends to think of it only in connection with homely chil-
dren and United States senators who have been defeated,
preferably in the primary, for reelection. Nonetheless, char-
acter—the willingness to accept responsibility for one's own
life—is the source from which self-respect springs.
    —Joan Didion, "On Self-Respect," from
      Slouching Towards Bethlehem

Staying sane in an insane world is a challenge we all
face. We live in troubled times in which everything seems to
be in flux. The values of the past are all being called into
question and being often foolishly discarded. It's been said
that the world has changed more in the past half century
than in all of previous history.

What has really happened? Are we living in a world of
eroding values, a world where ethics no longer apply, where

no one is willing to take responsibility for his or her actions—a world so fragmented by change that there is no connectedness? Have we broken through boundaries in the quest for freedom, only to find chaos? Was our greatest misconception the equation of human freedom with narcissistic indulgence and isolation, rather than connectedness to others.

Many people I meet are overwhelmed by anxiety, insecurity, and self-doubt—they feel alienated from themselves and from others. The old book of rules has been tossed out—those rules which required that we put duty before pleasure, that achievement came through hard work, that sex belonged rightfully in a committed relationship (preferably marriage), that it was important to finish the main course before gobbling up dessert. But in the war between the old and new values, some of us have become casualties. Some of us are out of control; feeling empty, we race about, "searching for ourselves."

Where is the freedom in all that? The truth is, there is none. Nor is there happiness. All of us have fantasies that can never be realized. Would that our bodies remained lithe forever; that stardom tap us on the shoulder; that others love us unconditionally. But this is pure adolescent fantasy, yet it traps many of us who fail to grow and realize the possibilities for enhancing our lives and the lives of those to whom we're connected.

Are we going to continue in this spiraling madness or get back to some sort of sane living? A choice has to be made. Can we once again embrace our traditional concepts of love, work, and family, and give meaning to our lives?

Everyone needs anchors in life: a balance that comes

from a broad definition of self including work, family, and ties to community.

Let me talk more about this concept of self. I know there are many things over which we have little or no control. However, I also know there are many things over which we do have control—more things, in fact, than we are often willing to admit. The ability to recognize those things over which we do have control is important to women who want to become autonomous.

It has been my goal in life to become an autonomous woman—a woman who needs little and desires much. The woman dominated by need will be dependent upon others to provide what she lacks or believes she lacks. But the woman motivated by desire is able to set her own goals, devise strategies for achieving them, and carry out those strategies. This is why I advocate autonomy. When you reach beyond neediness to commandeer desire, you reinforce your sense of self even as you strengthen your connections to others.

About three years ago, I had a talk with my attorney, Michael Stein. We were discussing how women viewed money more as if it were a gift, rather than a reward for their hard work. It is my belief that, in addition to a meaningful job or career, sound financial planning affords a woman a real measure of strength and independence. Quite simply, every woman should open an IRA—an Individual Retirement Account. This is a guaranteed social-security system, a safeguard against insolvency. If you're married, you may need one even more urgently. Consider depositing two thousand dollars a year into an IRA, under your name only, which your husband will be unable to touch. Should it happen, after twenty-three years, that your marriage falls apart, you've still got your account at the bank. By that time your two thousand dollars a year, accumulating interest all those years, will have multiplied to about a half-million dollars at the prevailing rate of interest. That's a lot of consolation, and it's all yours.

Michael and I also discussed women working together and the problems involved. "What women don't understand," Michael said, "is that men have always had a team on their side. Men have always had attorneys, personal accountants, contacts. They know who to go to when they want something, and how to transact business—personal or professional—over a drink. What matters now is that women, too, learn to build such teams. They're going to get shot down if they don't." It was some of the best advice I ever heard.

Finding women teammates, though, won't be easy. You must develop a few instincts. Are they trustworthy? Are they really rooting for you? Will they be available when you're at a low point, but not resent you when you're up? We've all grown up wanting female friends, but we've been taught that when push comes to shove, our best friends won't hesitate to run off with the man we love, cut us out of a job, or fail to defend us when we're under attack. I see women changing, becoming more caring and sensitive to each other, but still that old ingrained sense of competition insinuates itself. Women, for the most part, operate as free agents and the team be damned—it's what we learned at Mother's knee. We compete because we've been taught there can be only one winner—that is, only one woman can get the guy, only one woman can get the good job.

In these times, we have to function as a team, to learn to give and take. If we did, women would have power. We are, after all, fifty-two percent of the population. Do you know of any other majority treated as if it were a minority? Women are. Yet, sadly, it is women who encourage men to veto the ERA. If we are second-class citizens, women, more than men, today are responsible; women are holding other women down, sabotaging and denigrating each other by refusing to have on paper a single sentence affirming women's equal rights. Isn't *that* madness? Granted, the ERA is not going to change everything, but its failure to be ratified so far underscores something remarkable: We still don't trust ourselves or others like us. Characteristic of all minorities, this attitude is at the root of our negative self-image. Heeding too many negative messages about ourselves, we're insecure and feel that we're insignificant. But we're not! By defusing those negative messages and by developing self-esteem, we'll stop savaging ourselves. We *can* have what we want.

I learned one thing growing up in an Old World family: Women must fit into the customary pattern of all women before them. I said no to it. The first time I appeared on a television program (*The Mike Douglas Show*), my daughter was sixteen, my son twelve; I'd been married for seventeen years. I was on the air for the last five minutes of the show, during which time I was having words with Otto Preminger. When the show aired, I was in my den in Detroit and my mother was watching from her living room in New York. I called her when the show was over. "Well," I asked, "what did you think?" My mother's response was good news/bad news. "I liked your show," she said first. (I suppose Douglas's image didn't appear on her screen.) Then she asked, "When are you going to stay home and take care of your children?"

I'm not the only woman to face ambivalence about achievement by those who purport to care. But a long time ago I made my decision: I would make my own life valuable by doing something meaningful with it; I would live on my own terms, set my own course, pursue my own goals. Of course, I always cared about my family and their well-being. I have a supportive family team behind me and, truly, that's not a matter of luck. I dedicated myself over the years to trying to have them understand me and to constructing such a team. My children never had a full-time mother; my husband probably had dinner alone too often. Through it all, we remained close as a family. We always respected one another's goals. My son, Scott, who is now twenty-two years old, recently told me he wanted to marry a woman with a strong sense of herself, with interests and with a career: "I don't want to be responsible for bringing life home to a wife." Hearing that, I felt I'd succeeded as a parent, a mother, a friend.

As I've mentioned, there was a point early in my marriage when I supported my family. I didn't want to leave my children in the care of others to go to work, but I had no choice if we were to survive. I think back now on the baby-sitters I hired without knowing a thing about them, people who miraculously came through for us. I regret not having been with my children more when they were young and, truthfully, I gave my family, and myself, a hard time out of guilt. I was not being a "good" mother. Some of those days were maddening, totally frustrating, just out-and-out bad days.

Sometimes we experience bad days as if they will never end. During these bad days, we are dysfunctional, uneasy, fearful, careless, distracted. We believe we can't go on. But we can and we must. Here's how.

GETTING THROUGH THE BAD DAYS

Accept it: Bad days are inevitable. If we live seventy-five years, our lives will span 27,393 days, a number of which will be downers. These bad days may be the result of universally understandable setbacks: loss of a love, financial struggles, stretches of isolation and loneliness, irreconcilable conflicts with a spouse or a child. Or these bad days may be the result of less momentous reversals, which can still be met with understanding and sympathy by others; some examples are: flash fights with a spouse that cause sleepless nights, shops that are out of everything we want, insults from strangers on the street, rejections from those whose approval we seek, and any number of other everyday disappointments. As the heroine in Grace Paley's story, "An Interest in Life," comments with justifiable irritation: "My husband gave me a broom one Christmas. That wasn't right. No one can tell me it was meant kindly." Hers was definitely a bad day, and we needn't have been presented with a broom and dustpan ourselves to know why.

When bad days come in streaks, they seem to last, not a matter of days, but an eternity: Will the kids ever quiet down? Why, suddenly, do glasses slip from our fingers? Why do we trip up stairs? Why is dinner always a charred mess? Will our jobs ever be anything but monotonous? When will things go our way?

No one has misfortune licked. Certainly not me, certainly

not you. And if we trekked to some remote corner of the world to find a mystic who knows the Meaning of Life, I'd bet even he would confess to days of doubt, ennui, and spiritual discontent. No one can live in a thoroughly blissful state. What matters, though, is how we handle the bad days.

Let's take a look at how we perceive ourselves and others on bad days. There are three traps we must avoid: that of the perfectionist, the personalizer, and the victim.

Are you a perfectionist? The all-or-nothing approach to life places an insupportable burden on your back and on the backs of others. The striver sets realistic goals and then works hard to achieve them. She wants to be more than she is, she wants to better herself. She derives satisfaction from a task, then lets it go and moves on to something else. The perfectionist, though, wants to be *everything* at once. Crowded into a corner by details, she takes all mistakes on the chin. Mistakes prove to her that she's not good enough. Since her expectations are unrealistic to begin with, she is forever dissatisfied with herself and feels she must conceal her slip-ups from others. And because the perfectionist finds constant fault with herself, imagine the problems she creates in her relations with those "imperfect" others.

Those "others" are frequent disrupters of the perfectionist's tidy little world: "Don't walk on the carpet. I cleaned it just this morning." The perfectionist has a short fuse when life is not orderly. And because she is obsessed with details, she has difficulty completing anything: "I have to take that quilt apart again. It's not quite right." If you're spending too much of your time ensnared in details, demanding too much from yourself and from others, realize there is no perfect mate, no perfect life, no perfect place where the sun always shines. Mistakes are part of life. Learn to accept mistakes as just mistakes, not as proof that you "can't do anything right." When you can forgive your own mistakes and the mistakes of others, bad days will sail by. See things for what they are. The slightly overbaked apple pie should not cause as much commotion as the stove that blows up. The perfectionist lacks perspective. This is also a major problem for the personalizer.

Are you a personalizer? Can you distinguish between what actually occurs and how you *feel* about it? Do your emotions color all of your perceptions? When emotions run high, it is hard to be rational. When we are shocked, hurt, angry, or disappointed, we are all reduced to a bundle of raw nerves. But we must all learn to be analytical, which is easier to do if we remain calm and rational.

Consider Al and Betty. After leaving a party late on a snowy night, Al drives them home while Betty sits quietly fuming because Al had spent some time at the party talking to an old girl friend he hadn't seen in years. Al is in a great mood, though he dislikes driving in the snow, which is now falling heavily. Betty remains quiet. Al grows agitated. Finally, when Al asks her why he's getting the silent treatment, Betty lashes into him. Al makes a left turn and skids into a tree. Although Betty and Al are only mildly shaken up, and the car is barely scratched, Betty loses control. She accuses Al of trying to "kill" her. Al responds by calling her a jealous, nagging wife. Crying now, Betty says, "You don't love me." Al ignores this and accuses Betty of breaking his concentration on the treacherous roads. Eventually, inching along, this couple-at-odds arrives home.

Let's analyze what really happened here. What if Al had ignored his old girl friend? What might Betty have thought then? ("Why is Al pretending that Marcy doesn't exist? Is he acting nonchalant merely for appearances' sake?") Were Betty more of an *observer,* she'd have seen Al's encounter with Marcy as little more than an instance of two former lovers catching up on each other's lives. Al has never given Betty cause to doubt his fidelity. Why then did Betty feel so hurt? Is it that Betty feels she and Al aren't as close as they could be? Doesn't it have more to do with Betty's feelings of insecurity and her fear that something is lacking in their relationship? By calmly observing what took place, and by correctly interpreting it, Betty could have seen that Al's encounter with Marcy was not a threat to their relationship; instead, it could have served as a reminder that all relationships need constant renewal. It wouldn't have been such a bad day after all.

If Betty had kept events in perspective, if she had been able to keep some distance between what actually happened and her emotional reaction to it, if she had *not* personalized everything, she wouldn't have seen herself as helpless. In short, she wouldn't have seen herself as a victim. All victims see themselves as helpless.

Are you a victim? Does "everything happen to you"? The cashier at the supermarket shortchanges you. Your sister or brother or husband dumps her or his problems on you, virtually making you feel responsible for what has gone wrong. You're everyone's "best pal," but when it's time for you to rest your weary head and get some sympathy, you get the cold shoulder.

Victims hesitate to speak up or to assert or defend themselves. They worry that others won't like them. Instead of seeing themselves as nonassertive, they blame others, who always seem to ask too much of them. "If only . . ." says the victim. "If only I hadn't been there when . . ." "If only I weren't too old for . . ." "If only others would give me respect . . ." "If only life were better to me . . ."

Playing the victim is no fun. Victims are often psychologically paralyzed, and feel unable to do for themselves. One thing is for certain—no one can stop the clock. Wallowing in self-pity doesn't change anything. If you settle for wishful thinking about life changing for you, it will not get better. The "If only . . ." habit will keep you a procrastinator who will never achieve. You must make life work for you and give you what you desire. Do what you can for yourself. And do it *now*.

Bad days, after all, can be handled. Don't be fatalistic about them; don't dwell on them. If you do, you stand a good chance of falling into one of the three traps. You are in danger of making the mistake of the perfectionist in being obsessive, of the personalizer in being overly emotional, of the victim in being passive.

Don't elevate frustrations to the level of catastrophes. Most of them are merely irritations—treat them that way and you will find that even the grayest bad days will take on a rosier hue.

One of the main reasons I wrote *Men Are Just Desserts* is my belief that what happens to the individual woman, and what happens within her marriage and her family, affects society in general. For women to achieve happiness, we need interdependence, flexibility, and a sense of commitment. But if women are to have a sense of personal fulfillment and worth, we must be able to place ourselves at the center of our own lives. We must have a sense of emotional, financial, and career purpose and independence. This can be gained only through living by our own standards and setting our own goals. This is why I stress autonomy again and again.

To live autonomously and yet remain committed to others gives our lives balance and sanity in a world that seems increasingly insane. *Ms.* magazine called the 1980s the "decade of the woman." In many ways women have outdistanced men in social and emotional growth. But in so doing, we have alienated many men. Divisiveness gets us nowhere. It's not for us to prove we can do battle with men, using the same weapons against them they've used against us for centuries. Instead, we must all work together if we are to keep the world reasonably safe and sane. I know women have it within themselves to do it.

Sociologist Ashley Montagu said that we should "die young—late." This means we must keep ourselves open to life, growing *younger* in spirit as we grow older in years. We must take risks, we must never surrender our sense of adventure. Isn't that what being a woman is really all about? Isn't that what *you* can be all about?

I'm with you!

If you have found *Men Are Just Desserts* to be help-
ful and informative, and would like to consider taking a seminar with Dr. Friedman—or if you would
simply care to share your response to *Men Are Just
Desserts* with Dr. Friedman—please feel free to
write to her at the following address:

Dr. Sonya Friedman
111 South Woodward Avenue
Suite 250
Birmingham, Michigan 48011